Workbook

Science

PEARSON
Scott Foresman

Editorial Offices: Glenview, Illinois • Parsippany, New Jersey • New York, New York
Sales Offices: Needham, Massachusetts • Duluth, Georgia • Glenview, Illinois
Coppell, Texas • Sacramento, California • Mesa, Arizona

www.sfsuccessnet.com

Series Authors

Dr. Timothy Cooney
Professor of Earth Science and Science Education
University of Northern Iowa (UNI)
Cedar Falls, Iowa

Dr. Jim Cummins
Professor
Department of Curriculum, Teaching, and Learning
The University of Toronto
Toronto, Canada

Dr. James Flood
Distinguished Professor of Literacy and Language
School of Teacher Education
San Diego State University
San Diego, California

Barbara Kay Foots, M.Ed.
Science Education Consultant
Houston, Texas

Dr. M. Jenice Goldston
Associate Professor of Science Education
Department of Elementary Education Programs
University of Alabama
Tuscaloosa, Alabama

Dr. Shirley Gholston Key
Associate Professor of Science Education
Instruction and Curriculum Leadership
Department College of Education
University of Memphis
Memphis, Tennessee

Dr. Diane Lapp
Distinguished Professor of Reading and Language Arts in Teacher Education
San Diego State University
San Diego, California

Sheryl Mercier
Classroom Teacher
Dunlap Elementary School
Dunlap, California

Dr. Karen L. Ostlund
UTeach, College of Natural Sciences
The University of Texas at Austin
Austin, Texas

Dr. Nancy Romance
Professor of Science Education & Principal Investigator
NSF/IERI Science IDEAS Project
Charles E. Schmidt College of Science
Florida Atlantic University
Boca Raton, Florida

Dr. William Tate
Chair and Professor of Education and Applied Statistics
Department of Education
Washington University
St. Louis, Missouri

Dr. Kathryn C. Thornton
Professor
School of Engineering and Applied Science
University of Virginia
Charlottesville, Virginia

Dr. Leon Ukens
Professor of Science Education
Department of Physics, Astronomy, and Geosciences
Towson University
Towson, Maryland

Steve Weinberg
Consultant
Connecticut Center for Advanced Technology
East Hartford, Connecticut

Consulting Author

Dr. Michael P. Klentschy
Superintendent
El Centro Elementary School District
El Centro, California

ISBN: 0-328-12610-1
ISBN: 0-328-20064-6

Copyright © Pearson Education, Inc.
All Rights Reserved. Printed in the United States of America. This publication is protected by Copyright, and permission should be obtained from the publisher prior to any prohibited reproduction, storage in a retrieval system, or transmission in any form by any means, electronic, mechanical, photocopying, recording, or likewise. For information regarding permission(s), write to: Permissions Department, Scott Foresman, 1900 East Lake Avenue, Glenview, Illinois 60025.

7 8 9 10 V084 13 12 11 10 09 08 07 06

Unit A
Life Science

Chapter 1 • Living and Nonliving
Vocabulary Preview 1
How to Read Science 2
Lesson 1 . . . . 4, 4A
Lesson 2 . . . . 5, 5A
Lesson 3 . . . . 6, 6A
Lesson 4 . . . . 7, 7A
Math in Science 8
Take-Home Booklet 9
Using Science Pictures 135

Chapter 2 • Habitats
Vocabulary Preview 11
How to Read Science 12
Lesson 1 . . . . 14, 14A
Lesson 2 . . . . 15, 15A
Lesson 3 . . . . 16, 16A
Lesson 4 . . . . 17, 17A
Math in Science 18
Take-Home Booklet 19
Using Science Pictures 136

Chapter 3 • How Plants and Animals Live
Vocabulary Preview 21
How to Read Science 22
Lesson 1 . . . . 24, 24A
Lesson 2 . . . . 25, 25A
Lesson 3 . . . . 26, 26A
Lesson 4 . . . . 27, 27A
Lesson 5 . . . . 28, 28A
Math in Science 29
Take-Home Booklet 31
Using Science Pictures 137

Chapter 4 • Life Cycles
Vocabulary Preview 33
How to Read Science 34
Lesson 1 . . . . 36, 36A
Lesson 2 . . . . 37, 37A
Lesson 3 . . . . 38, 38A
Lesson 4 . . . . 39, 39A
Lesson 5 . . . . 40, 40A
Lesson 6 . . . . 41, 41A
Math in Science 42
Take-Home Booklet 43
Using Science Pictures 138

© Pearson Education, Inc.

Unit B
Earth Science

Chapter 5 • Food Chains

Vocabulary Preview 45
How to Read Science 46
Lesson 1 . . . . 48, 48A
Lesson 2 . . . . 49, 49A
Lesson 3 . . . . 50, 50A
Math in Science 51
Take-Home Booklet 53
Using Science Pictures 139

Chapter 6 • Land, Water, and Air

Vocabulary Preview 55
How to Read Science 56
Lesson 1 . . . . 58, 58A
Lesson 2 . . . . 59, 59A
Lesson 3 . . . . 60, 60A
Lesson 4 . . . . 61, 61A
Lesson 5 . . . . 62, 62A
Math in Science 63
Take-Home Booklet 65
Using Science Pictures 140

Chapter 7 • Weather

Vocabulary Preview 67
How to Read Science 68
Lesson 1 . . . . 70, 70A
Lesson 2 . . . . 71, 71A
Lesson 3 . . . . 72, 72A
Lesson 4 . . . . 73, 73A
Math in Science 74
Take-Home Booklet 75
Using Science Pictures 141

Unit C
Physical Science

Chapter 8 • Observing Matter

Vocabulary Preview 77
How to Read Science 78
Lesson 1 . . . . 80, 80A
Lesson 2 . . . . 81, 81A
Lesson 3 . . . . 82, 82A
Lesson 4 . . . . 83, 83A
Lesson 5 . . . . 84, 84A
Math in Science 85
Take-Home Booklet 87
Using Science Pictures 142

© Pearson Education, Inc.

Unit D
Space and Technology

Chapter 9 • Movement and Sound

Vocabulary Preview 89
How to Read Science 90
Lesson 1. . . . . 92, 92A
Lesson 2. . . . . 93, 93A
Lesson 3. . . . . 94, 94A
Lesson 4. . . . . 95, 95A
Lesson 5. . . . . 96, 96A
Lesson 6. . . . . 97, 97A
Math in Science 98
Take-Home Booklet 99
Using Science Pictures 143

Chapter 10 • Learning About Energy

Vocabulary Preview 101
How to Read Science 102
Lesson 1. . . . . 104, 104A
Lesson 2. . . . . 105, 105A
Lesson 3. . . . . 106, 106A
Lesson 4. . . . . 107, 107A
Lesson 5. . . . . 108, 108A
Math in Science 109
Take-Home Booklet 111
Using Science Pictures 144

Chapter 11 • Day and Night Sky

Vocabulary Preview 113
How to Read Science 114
Lesson 1. . . . . 116, 116A
Lesson 2. . . . . 117, 117A
Lesson 3. . . . . 118, 118A
Math in Science 119
Take-Home Booklet 121
Using Science Pictures 145

Chapter 12 • Science in Our World

Vocabulary Preview 123
How to Read Science 124
Lesson 1. . . . . 126, 126A
Lesson 2. . . . . 127, 127A
Lesson 3. . . . . 128, 128A
Lesson 4. . . . . 129, 129A
Lesson 5. . . . . 130, 130A
Lesson 6. . . . . 131, 131A
Math in Science 132
Take-Home Booklet 133
Using Science Pictures 146

GRADE 1 WORKBOOK

Photo Credits

Every effort has been made to secure permission and provide appropriate credit for photographic material. The publisher deeply regrets any omission and pledges to correct errors called to its attention in subsequent editions.
Unless otherwise acknowledged, all photographs are the property of Scott Foresman, a division of Pearson Education.
Photo locators denoted as follows: Top (T), Center (C), Bottom (B), Left (L), Right (R) Background (Bkgd)

135 ©Darrell Gulin/Corbis, ©Dan Guravich/Corbis
136 Daniel J. Cox/Natural Exposures, Digital Vision, David Samuel Robbins/Corbis, ©Yva Momatiuk/John Eastcott/Minden Pictures
137 Helen Williams/Photo Researchers, Inc., ©DK Images
138 ©George D. Lepp/Corbis, ©DK Images
139 ©Michael & Patricia Fogden/Corbis, ©Kevin Schafer/NHPA Limited
140 ©James Havey/Index Stock Imagery, ©Steve Dunwell/Getty Images
141 ©Stone/Getty Images, ©Bruce Peebles/Corbis
144 Getty Images
145 ©Roger Ressmeyer/Corbis, ©Jerry Lodriguss/Photo Researchers, Inc., ©Jet Propulsion Laboratory/NASA
146 ©Michael S. Yamashita/Corbis, ©J. Jangoux/Photo Researchers, Inc.

© Pearson Education, Inc.

Name ______________________________

Draw a picture to go with each word.

living

shelter

nonliving

© Pearson Education, Inc.

Directions: Read the words and draw pictures to illustrate them. Cut out the boxes to use as word cards.
Home Activity: Look around your home. Help your child use the word cards *living* and *nonliving* to label living and nonliving things in your home.

Name ______________________________

Use with Chapter 1.

Alike and Different

Observe. Look at the tree and the bear.

Apply It!

Use the chart on the next page. Tell how the tree and the bear are alike and different.

© Pearson Education, Inc.

Name ______________________

Use with Chapter 1.

Alike	Different

© Pearson Education, Inc.

Directions: Talk about how the tree and the bear are alike and different. Draw or write your answer to each question in the box.
Home Activity: Your child learned about the concept of alike and different. Name the following pairs and have your child tell one way the two are alike and one way they are different: Real cat and toy cat, dog and sunflower.

Notes

Name ______________________________

Use with pages 7–9.

What are living things?

Before You Read Lesson 1

Read each sentence. Do you think it is true? Do you think it is not true? Circle the word or words after each sentence that tell what you think.

1. Animals, plants, and people are living things.	True	Not True
2. Animals grow and change.	True	Not True
3. Plants cannot grow and change.	True	Not True

After You Read Lesson 1

Read each sentence again. Circle the word or words after each sentence that tell what you think now. Did you change any answers? Put an **X** by each answer that you changed.

1. Animals, plants, and people are living things.	True	Not True
2. Animals grow and change.	True	Not True
3. Plants cannot grow and change.	True	Not True

© Pearson Education, Inc.

Home Activity: Together talk about your child's answers. Have your child explain why his or her answers may have changed after reading the lesson.

Name ______________________________

Lesson 1 Review

Use with pages 7–9.

Complete the Sentence

Write the word that completes each sentence.

grow	change	living	move

1. Plants and animals are ______________ things.

2. Plants and animals ______________ bigger.

3. Animals ______________ on their own.

4. Plants ______________ and become different.

Alike and Different

5. Write the things that tell how plants and animals are alike and different.

can grow   can move   can change

Plants	Animals

© Scott Foresman

Name ______________________________

Use with pages 10–11.

What do plants need?

Before You Read Lesson 2

Read each sentence. Do you think it is true? Do you think it is not true? Circle the word or words after each sentence that tell what you think.

1. A need is something a living thing must have to live.	True	Not True
2. Plants need water and light.	True	Not True
3. Plants do not need air.	True	Not True

After You Read Lesson 2

Read each sentence again. Circle the word or words after each sentence that tell what you think now. Did you change any answers? Put an **X** by each answer that you changed.

1. A need is something a living thing must have to live.	True	Not True
2. Plants need water and light.	True	Not True
3. Plants do not need air.	True	Not True

© Pearson Education, Inc.

Home Activity: Together talk about your child's answers. Have your child explain why his or her answers may have changed after reading the lesson.

Name ______________________________

Use with pages 10–11.

Complete the Sentence

Write the word that completes each sentence.
Use each word twice.

grow	living

1. An animal is a ______________ thing.

2. A plant is a ______________ thing.

3. A plant can ______________.

4. An animal can ______________.

Draw Conclusions

5. What are things plants need?

________ ________ ________ ________

© Scott Foresman

Name ______________________________

Use with pages 12–13.

What do animals need?

Before You Read Lesson 3

Read each sentence. Do you think it is true? Do you think it is not true? Circle the word or words after each sentence that tell what you think.

1.	Animals need water.	True	Not True
2.	Animals do not need space to live.	True	Not True
3.	Animals need shelter, or a safe place.	True	Not True

After You Read Lesson 3

Read each sentence again. Circle the word or words after each sentence that tell what you think now. Did you change any answers? Put an **X** by each answer that you changed.

1.	Animals need water.	True	Not True
2.	Animals do not need space to live.	True	Not True
3.	Animals need shelter, or a safe place.	True	Not True

© Pearson Education, Inc.

Home Activity: Together talk about your child's answers. Have your child explain why his or her answers may have changed after reading the lesson.

Name ______________________

Use with pages 12–13.

Complete the Sentence

Write the word that completes each sentence.

air	shelter	food	water

1. A bird's ____________ is a nest.

2. Animals drink ____________.

3. Animals eat ____________.

4. Animals use ____________.

Alike and Different

5. Write the things that tell how the needs of plants and animals are alike and different.

needs air   needs shelter   needs the Sun   needs water

Plants	Animals

© Scott Foresman

Name ____________________________________

Use with pages 14–17.

What are nonliving things?

Before You Read Lesson 4

Read each sentence. Do you think it is true? Do you think it is not true? Circle the word or words after each sentence that tell what you think.

1. Nonliving things used to be alive but aren't alive now.	True	Not True
2. Nonliving things do not grow and change.	True	Not True
3. A rock is a nonliving thing.	True	Not True

After You Read Lesson 4

Read each sentence again. Circle the word or words after each sentence that tell what you think now. Did you change any answers? Put an **X** by each answer that you changed.

1. Nonliving things used to be alive but aren't alive now.	True	Not True
2. Nonliving things do not grow and change.	True	Not True
3. A rock is a nonliving thing.	True	Not True

© Pearson Education, Inc.

Home Activity: Together talk about your child's answers. Have your child explain why his or her answers may have changed after reading the lesson.

Name ____________________

Use with pages 14–17.

Complete the Sentence

Write the word that completes each sentence.

alive	book	grow	air

1. A ____________ is a nonliving thing.

2. Nonliving things cannot ____________.

3. A nonliving thing does not need ____________.

4. A nonliving thing is not ____________.

Draw Conclusions

5. Look at the picture. Write three things that are nonliving.

____________ ____________ ____________

© Scott Foresman

Name ______________________________

Sorting and Counting Animals and Plants

Look at these pictures.

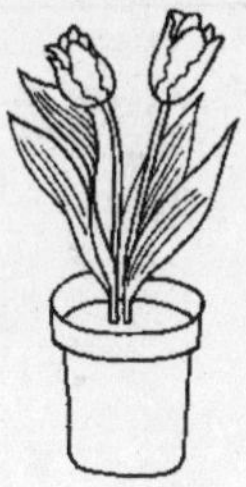

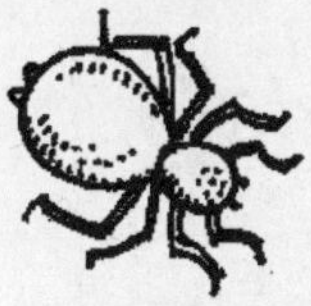
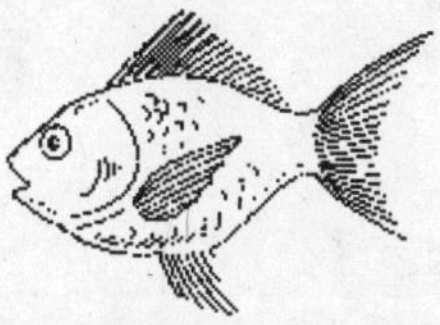

Put a ✓ by each animal.

Put an X by each plant.

Count the ✓s. Write the number. ______

Count the Xs. Write the number. ______

© Pearson Education, Inc.

Directions: Read the directions. Draw the ✓s and Xs. Then count and write the number of ✓s and the number of Xs.
Home Activity: Your child learned how to sort and count animals and plants. Ask your child to explain what he or she did on the page.

Notes

Family Science Activity

Adventure Walk

Materials
- paper
- crayons
- small sticky notes

Steps
1. Go on a walk with your child around the neighborhood.
2. Ask your child to point out any living things on your walk.
3. Then ask your child to point out any nonliving things.
4. Encourage your child to tell how the living things are different from the nonliving things. Have your child describe the needs of a living thing he or she points out.
5. When you return home, invite your child to draw a picture of some of the things you both saw on your walk.
6. Hang the picture in a central area where your child can refer to it. Later in the week, give your child small sticky notes with the labels "living" or "nonliving." Have your child stick the appropriate label over different things on the picture.

© Pearson Education, Inc.

Take Home Booklet

Use with Chapter 1

Dear Family,

In the science chapter Living and Nonliving, your child is learning the differences between living and nonliving things. Our class has learned that plants and animals are living things. We have also learned that plants and animals have needs that they must have to live. The children have also investigated how some nonliving things are made to look like living things.

While learning about living and nonliving things, the children have also learned many new vocabulary words. Help your child to make these words a part of his or her own vocabulary by using them when you talk together about living and nonliving things.

living
shelter
nonliving

These following pages include activities that you and your child can do together. By participating in your child's education, you will help to bring the learning home.

Look at the pictures and words below.
Label each picture using a word from the box.

living
nonliving
shelter

____________ ____________ ____________

Fun Fact

Birds are the only living things with feathers. Birds use feathers to fly. They also use feathers to keep warm and dry. Feathers are very light. Feathers help birds live.

© Pearson Education, Inc.

Animals and Plants

Color the pictures of the tree and tiger.
Write what the plant needs to live.
Write what the animal needs to live.

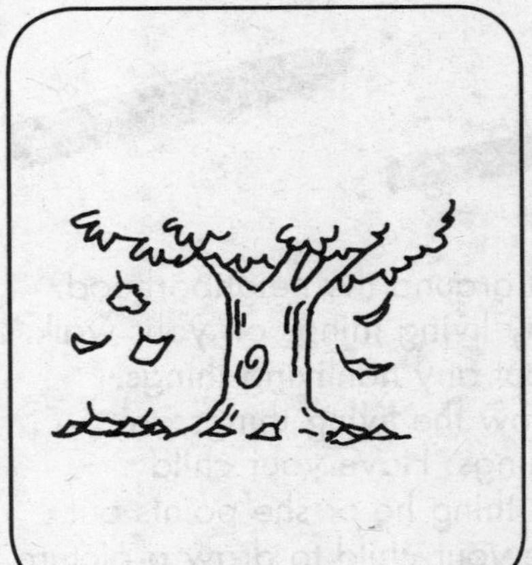

____________ ____________

____________ ____________

____________ ____________

Name ______________________________

Use with Chapter 2.

Draw a picture to go with each word.

habitat

forest

wetland

ocean

desert

© Pearson Education, Inc.

Directions: Read the words and draw pictures to illustrate them. Cut out the boxes to use as word cards.
Home Activity: Review the word cards *forest, wetland, ocean,* and *desert* with your child. Talk about the animals and plants that might live in that kind of habitat.

Name ________________________________

Use with Chapter 2.

Picture Clues

TARGET SKILL

Read the science story.
Look at the picture.
Answer the question.

Forest
Many birds live in the forest. They build nests in the trees. They live in the nests.

Apply It!

Use the chart on the next page.
Observe What is the bird using to build the nest?
Look for clues in the picture.

© Pearson Education, Inc.

Name ____________________

Use with Chapter 2.

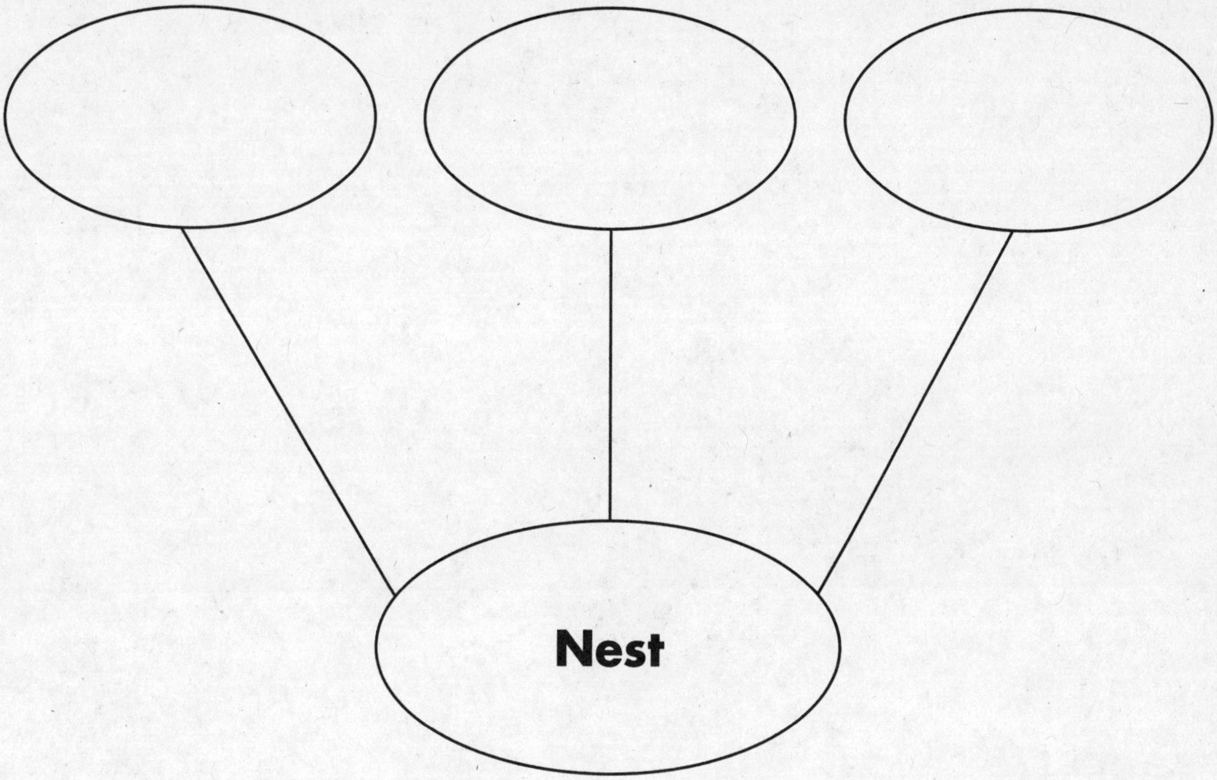

© Pearson Education, Inc.

Directions: Read the science story and look at the picture. Use what you see in the picture to help you answer the question.
Home Activity: Your child practiced the science skill of observing picture clues. Find a magazine or newspaper picture that has lots of details and ask your child to describe what he or she sees in the picture.

Notes

Name ______________________________

Use with pages 31–33.

What is a forest habitat?

Before You Read Lesson 1

Read each sentence. Do you think it is true? Do you think it is not true? Circle the word or words after each sentence that tell what you think.

1.	Animals and plants live in a habitat.	True	Not True
2.	A habitat gives animals and plants what they need to live.	True	Not True
3.	A forest has very few plants.	True	Not True

After You Read Lesson 1

Read each sentence again. Circle the word or words after each sentence that tell what you think now. Did you change any answers? Put an **X** by each answer that you changed.

1.	Animals and plants live in a habitat.	True	Not True
2.	A habitat gives animals and plants what they need to live.	True	Not True
3.	A forest has very few plants.	True	Not True

© Pearson Education, Inc.

Home Activity: Together talk about your child's answers. Have your child explain why his or her answers may have changed after reading the lesson.

Name ______________________________

Use with pages 31–33.

Complete the Sentence

Write the word that completes each sentence.

winter	habitat	summer	forest

1. Plants and animals find shelter in a ____________.

2. A ____________ is a place with many trees.

3. Plants and animals get what they need in the ____________.

4. Many plants do not grow in the ____________.

Picture Clues

5. Use picture clues to find the forest habitat. Color the picture of the forest habitat.

© Scott Foresman

Name ______________________________

Use with pages 34–35.

What is a wetland habitat?

Before You Read Lesson 2

Read each sentence. Do you think it is true? Do you think it is not true? Circle the word or words after each sentence that tell what you think.

1. A wetland is a habitat that has lots of water.	True	Not True
2. Only plants live in wetlands.	True	Not True
3. A wetland gets lots of rain in summer.	True	Not True

After You Read Lesson 2

Read each sentence again. Circle the word or words after each sentence that tell what you think now. Did you change any answers? Put an **X** by each answer that you changed.

1. A wetland is a habitat that has lots of water.	True	Not True
2. Only plants live in wetlands.	True	Not True
3. A wetland gets lots of rain in summer.	True	Not True

© Pearson Education, Inc.

Home Activity: Together talk about your child's answers. Have your child explain why his or her answers may have changed after reading the lesson.

Name ____________________

Lesson 2 Review

Use with pages 34–35.

Complete the Sentence

Write the word that completes each sentence.

rain	Sun	wetland	frog

1. A habitat covered in water is a ____________.

2. There is a lot of ____________ in this habitat.

3. A ____________ lives in this habitat.

4. The ____________ shines in this habitat to help the plants grow.

Draw Conclusions

5. Circle the animal that lives in a wetland.

© Scott Foresman

Name ______________________________

Use with pages 36–37.

What is an ocean habitat?

Before You Read Lesson 3

Read each sentence. Do you think it is true? Do you think it is not true? Circle the word or words after each sentence that tell what you think.

1. An ocean is a habitat that has lots of water.	True	Not True
2. An ocean has salt water.	True	Not True
3. Only animals can live in the ocean.	True	Not True

After You Read Lesson 3

Read each sentence again. Circle the word or words after each sentence that tell what you think now. Did you change any answers? Put an **X** by each answer that you changed.

1. An ocean is a habitat that has lots of water.	True	Not True
2. An ocean has salt water.	True	Not True
3. Only animals can live in the ocean.	True	Not True

© Pearson Education, Inc.

Home Activity: Together talk about your child's answers. Have your child explain why his or her answers may have changed after reading the lesson.

Name ______________________________

Use with pages 36–37.

Complete the Sentence

Write the word or phrase that completes each sentence.

large	fish	ocean	salt water

1. The ______________ is a kind of habitat.

2. This habitat is very ______________.

3. There are ______________ living in this habitat.

4. The water in this habitat is ______________.

Picture Clues

5. Use picture clues to tell two things about an ocean habitat.

______________________ ______________________

© Scott Foresman

Name ______________________________

Use with pages 38–39.

What is a desert habitat?

Before You Read Lesson 4

Read each sentence. Do you think it is true? Do you think it is not true? Circle the word or words after each sentence that tell what you think.

1.	A desert is a very wet habitat.	True	Not True
2.	A cactus is a plant found in the desert.	True	Not True
3.	A desert is usually hot.	True	Not True

After You Read Lesson 4

Read each sentence again. Circle the word or words after each sentence that tell what you think now. Did you change any answers? Put an **X** by each answer that you changed.

1.	A desert is a very wet habitat.	True	Not True
2.	A cactus is a plant found in the desert.	True	Not True
3.	A desert is usually hot.	True	Not True

© Pearson Education, Inc.

Home Activity: Together talk about your child's answers. Have your child explain why his or her answers may have changed after reading the lesson.

Name ______________________________

Use with pages 38–39.

Complete the Sentence

Write the word that completes each sentence.

cactus	camel	hot	desert

1. A habitat with little water is a ____________.

2. It can be very ____________ in this habitat.

3. A ____________ is a plant that lives in this habitat.

4. An animal that lives in this habitat is a ____________.

Alike and Different

5. Write the things that tell how a wetland and a desert are alike and different.

is hot   gets sunlight   rains a lot   has plants and animals

Wetland	Desert

© Scott Foresman

Name ______________________________

Use with Chapter 2.

Counting Plants

Count the plants in the ocean picture.
Count the plants in the wetland picture.
Fill in the tally chart.

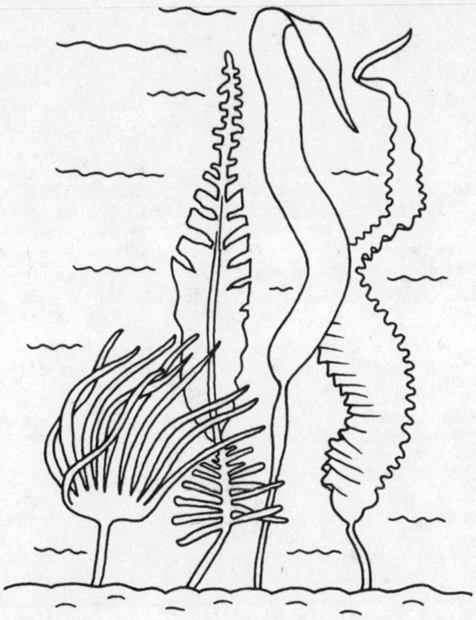

ocean

wetland

ocean	**wetland**

Which picture shows more plants?
Use the tally chart to answer the question.

© Pearson Education, Inc.

Directions: Look at each picture. For each plant you see, draw a tally mark in the correct place on the tally chart. Then count the tally marks and answer the question.
Home Activity: Your child learned how to fill in a tally chart. Ask your child to explain what he or she did on the page.

Notes

Family Science Activity

Habitat Diorama

Materials
- shoe box
- construction paper
- glue
- markers
- scissors
- natural items such as small rocks, leaves, and twigs

Steps
1. Explain to your child that a diorama is like a stage. It shows a small version of something real. Ask your child to make a diorama showing a local habitat.
2. First work with your child to create a background for the diorama using art supplies.
3. Next have your child make cut out animals to glue inside the diorama.
4. Complete the diorama using some natural items found outside, such as small rocks, leaves, or twigs.
5. Have children show and explain their dioramas to other family members.

© Pearson Education, Inc.

Use with Chapter 2

Dear Family,

In the science chapter Habitats, your child has learned about the different kinds of habitats animals live in. Our class has learned that habitats are places where plants and animals live. We have explored forests, wetlands, oceans, and deserts. While exploring these habitats, the children have learned about the types of animals that live in each habitat.

While learning about habitats, the children have also learned many new vocabulary words. Help your child to make these words a part of his or her own vocabulary by using them when you talk together about habitats.

habitat
forest
wetland
ocean
desert

These following pages include activities that you and your child can do together. By participating in your child's education, you will help to bring the learning home.

Habitat Riddles

Read the riddles.
Draw a line from the riddle to the type of habitat described.

It is very dry. It gets a lot of sunlight. A cactus can live there.	
It is covered with water. There is a lot of rain in the summer. Dragonflies and ducks live there.	
It is large and deep. It has salt water. Whales live there.	
In the summer the trees have many leaves. In the winter, the trees lose their leaves. Black bears and raccoons live there.	

Fun Fact

Did you know polar bears live in the desert? Polar bears live in the arctic desert. The arctic desert is covered with ice. But it only gets a little rain each year.

© Pearson Education, Inc.

Name the Habitat

Look at the habitat pictures.
Label each picture using a word from the word box.
Color the pictures.

ocean	desert
forest	wetland

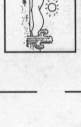

____

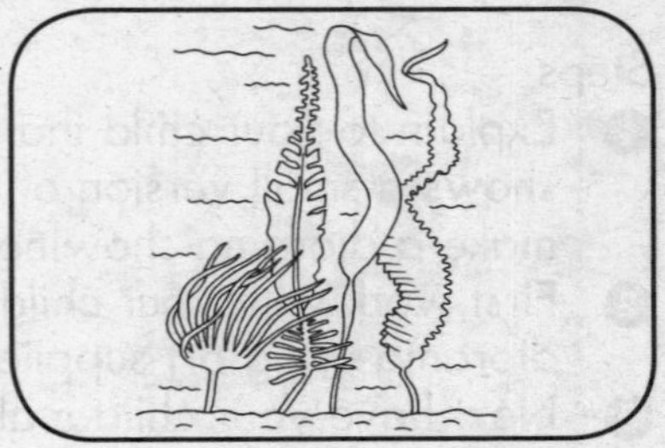

____

____

____

Name ______________________________

Vocabulary Preview

Use with Chapter 3.

Draw a picture to go with each word.

camouflage

root

antennae

flower

stem

leaf

Directions: Read the words and draw pictures to illustrate them. Cut out the boxes to use as word cards.
Home Activity: Find and show a picture of a flower. Ask your child to choose the word cards that tell about the flower and its parts *(flower, root, leaf, stem)*.

© Pearson Education, Inc.

Name ______________________________

Use with Chapter 3.

Alike and Different

Observe. Look at the leaves on the plants.

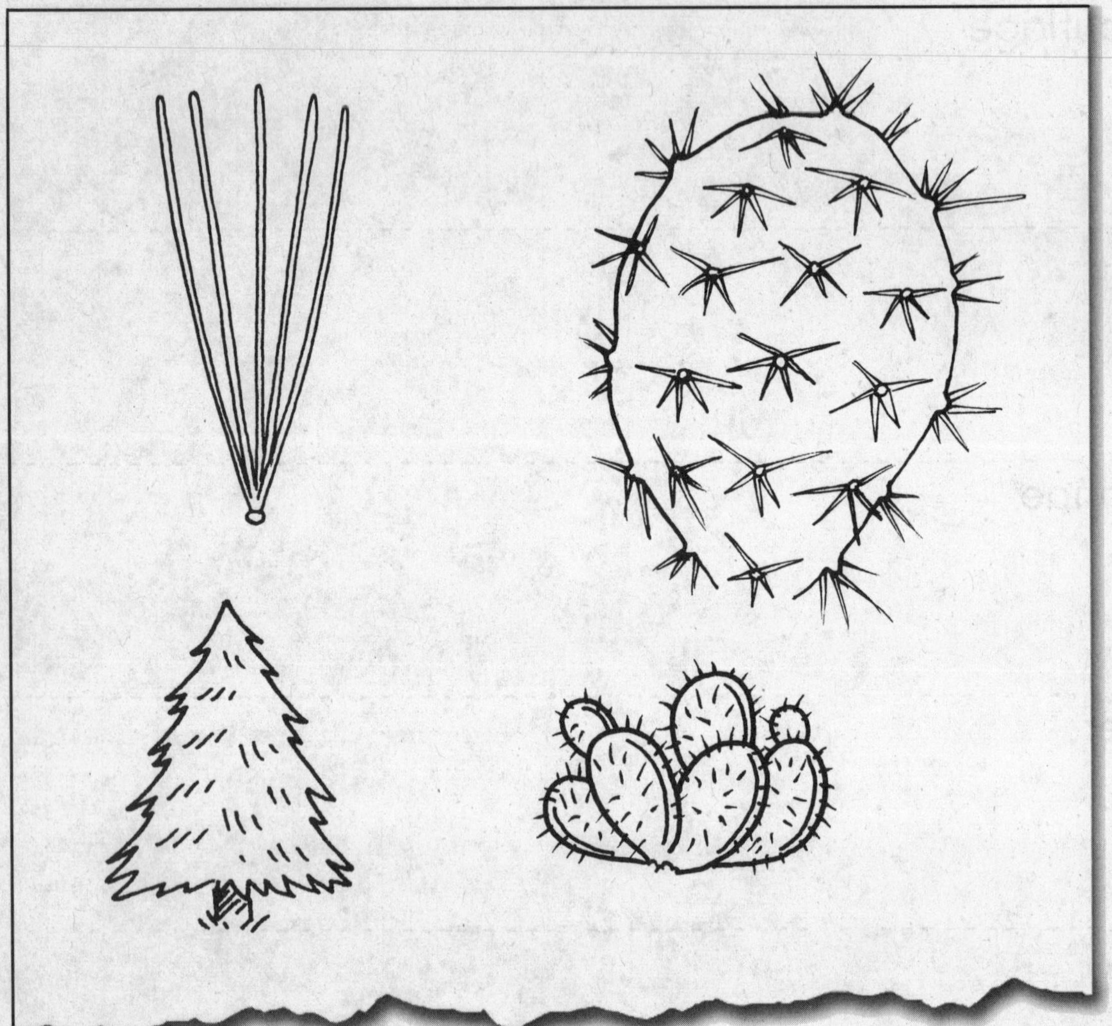

Apply It!

Use the chart on the next page. Tell how the leaves on the plant are alike and different.

© Pearson Education, Inc.

Name ______________________________

Alike	Different

Directions: Talk about how the leaves on the pine tree and the cactus are alike and different. Draw or write your answer to each question in the box.
Home Activity: Your child learned about the concept of alike and different. Name the following pairs and have your child tell one way the two are alike and one way they are different: cat and fish, oak tree and rosebush.

© Pearson Education, Inc.

Notes

Name ______________________

Use with pages 55–57.

What helps animals live in their habitats?

Before You Read Lesson 1

Read each sentence. Do you think it is true? Do you think it is not true? Circle the word or words after each sentence that tell what you think.

1. Fur helps a mountain goat live in a cold habitat.	True	Not True
2. Antennae help a crab walk.	True	Not True
3. Fins help a clownfish swim in water.	True	Not True

After You Read Lesson 1

Read each sentence again. Circle the word or words after each sentence that tell what you think now. Did you change any answers? Put an **X** by each answer that you changed.

1. Fur helps a mountain goat live in a cold habitat.	True	Not True
2. Antennae help a crab walk.	True	Not True
3. Fins help a clownfish swim in water.	True	Not True

© Pearson Education, Inc.

Home Activity: Together talk about your child's answers. Have your child explain why his or her answers may have changed after reading the lesson.

Name ___________________________

Use with pages 55–57.

Complete the Sentence

Write the word that completes each sentence.

antennae	fins	fur	shell

1. A crab uses ______________ to feel what is around it.

2. To swim, a fish needs ______________.

3. A goat's ______________ helps it stay warm.

4. A ______________ keeps a hermit crab safe.

Picture Clues

5. Use picture clues to tell what body parts help the lobster live in its habitat. Write the body parts in the circles.

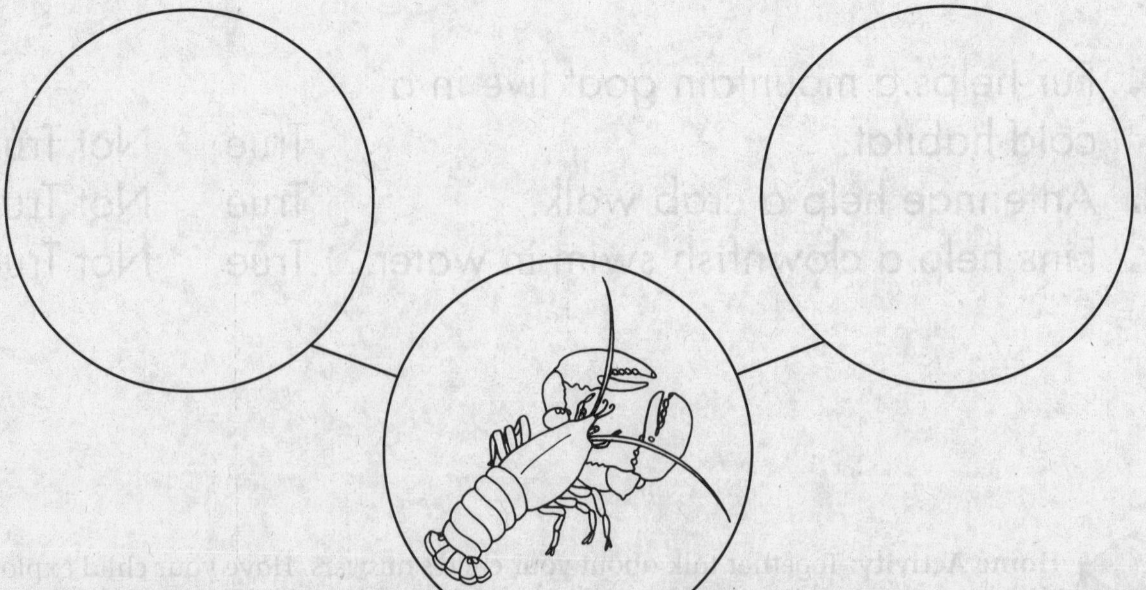

© Scott Foresman

Name ______________________________

Use with pages 58–61.

How do animals get food?

Before You Read Lesson 2

Read each sentence. Do you think it is true? Do you think it is not true? Circle the word or words after each sentence that tell what you think.

1. Birds use wings to eat food.	True	Not True
2. Some birds eat seeds, and some birds eat meat.	True	Not True
3. A lion uses its claws to catch other animals.	True	Not True

After You Read Lesson 2

Read each sentence again. Circle the word or words after each sentence that tell what you think now. Did you change any answers? Put an **X** by each answer that you changed.

1. Birds use wings to eat food.	True	Not True
2. Some birds eat seeds, and some birds eat meat.	True	Not True
3. A lion uses its claws to catch other animals.	True	Not True

© Pearson Education, Inc.

Home Activity: Together talk about your child's answers. Have your child explain why his or her answers may have changed after reading the lesson.

Name ________________________

Use with pages 58–61.

Complete the Sentence

Write the word that completes each sentence.

claws	hump	chew	beak

1. A bird uses a ____________ to eat its food.

2. When there is no food or water, a camel's ____________ helps it live.

3. Some animals use sharp ____________ to catch food.

4. Many animals use teeth to ____________ their food.

Alike and Different

5. Write about ways that birds and giraffes get and eat food that are alike and different.

use wings   use teeth   use a long neck   use a beak

Birds	Giraffes

© Scott Foresman

Name ______________________________ **Think, Read, Learn**

Use with pages 62–67.

What can help protect animals?

Before You Read Lesson 3

Read each sentence. Do you think it is true? Do you think it is not true? Circle the word or words after each sentence that tell what you think.

1. Camouflage makes an animal or plant hard to see.	True	Not True
2. Crocodiles live in the water.	True	Not True
3. A kangaroo makes a loud call when there is danger.	True	Not True

After You Read Lesson 3

Read each sentence again. Circle the word or words after each sentence that tell what you think now. Did you change any answers? Put an **X** by each answer that you changed.

1. Camouflage makes an animal or plant hard to see.	True	Not True
2. Crocodiles live in the water.	True	Not True
3. A kangaroo makes a loud call when there is danger.	True	Not True

© Pearson Education, Inc.

Home Activity: Together talk about your child's answers. Have your child explain why his or her answers may have changed after reading the lesson.

Name ______________________

Use with pages 62–67.

Complete the Sentence

Write the word that completes each sentence.

hide	camouflage	ears	tail

1. Some plants and animals use ____________ to make them hard to see.

2. An animal's color can help it ____________.

3. A deer uses its ____________ to tell about danger.

4. Some animals use their ____________ to listen for sounds.

Predict

5. Predict where the katydid would hide from danger. Draw a picture of what you predict.

I know	I predict
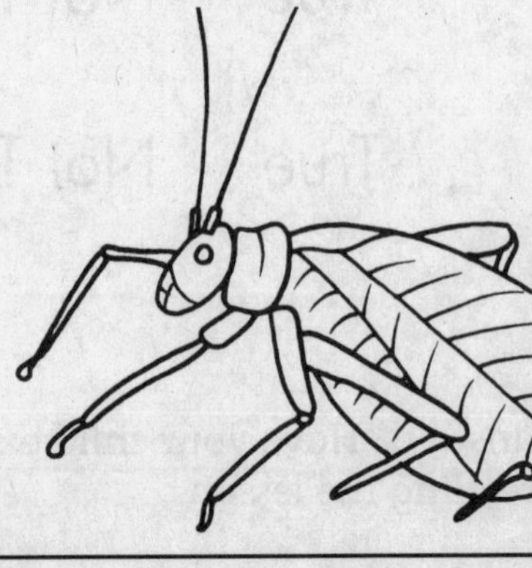	

© Scott Foresman

Name ______________________________

Use with pages 68–71.

What are some parts of plants?

Before You Read Lesson 4

Read each sentence. Do you think it is true? Do you think it is not true? Circle the word or words after each sentence that tell what you think.

1. A flower makes food for a plant.	True	Not True
2. A stem is a part of a plant.	True	Not True
3. Leaves have different shapes.	True	Not True

After You Read Lesson 4

Read each sentence again. Circle the word or words after each sentence that tell what you think now. Did you change any answers? Put an **X** by each answer that you changed.

1. A flower makes food for a plant.	True	Not True
2. A stem is a part of a plant.	True	Not True
3. Leaves have different shapes.	True	Not True

© Pearson Education, Inc.

Home Activity: Together talk about your child's answers. Have your child explain why his or her answers may have changed after reading the lesson.

Name ______________________

Use with pages 68–71.

Complete the Sentence

Write the word that completes each sentence.

flower	root	leaf	stem

1. A plant's food is made in a __________.

2. The __________ helps a plant get water.

3. A __________ makes seeds for the plant.

4. A rose has thorns on its __________ to keep it safe.

Important Details

5. Look at the picture and write three important details about it.

__________ __________ __________

© Scott Foresman

Name ______________________________

Use with pages 72–73.

What helps protect plants?

Before You Read Lesson 5

Read each sentence. Do you think it is true? Do you think it is not true? Circle the word or words after each sentence that tell what you think.

1.	Spines look and feel like sharp pins.	True	Not True
2.	Stone plants hide their roots, stems, and flowers.	True	Not True
3.	Only animals use camouflage.	True	Not True

After You Read Lesson 5

Read each sentence again. Circle the word or words after each sentence that tell what you think now. Did you change any answers? Put an **X** by each answer that you changed.

1.	Spines look and feel like sharp pins.	True	Not True
2.	Stone plants hide their roots, stems, and flowers.	True	Not True
3.	Only animals use camouflage.	True	Not True

© Pearson Education, Inc.

Home Activity: Together talk about your child's answers. Have your child explain why his or her answers may have changed after reading the lesson.

Name ______________________

Use with pages 72–73.

Complete the Sentence

Write the word that completes each sentence.

stems	camouflage	leaves	spines

1. Plants can have ____________ on them to keep them safe.

2. You can only see the ____________ on some plants.

3. Some plants use ____________ to stay safe.

4. Plants can hide their ____________ in the ground.

Alike and Different

5. Write one thing about how the plants are alike and one thing about how they are different.

Alike: ______________________________

Different: ______________________________

© Scott Foresman

Name ______________________________

Use with Chapter 3.

Classify Animals

Look at the groups of animals.
Tell how the animals in a group are alike.
Then count the animals in each group.
Use >, <, or = to compare the two groups.

Directions: Look at the animals in each group. Tell how the animals in the group are alike. Are they big or small? Do they have fur or feathers? Do they swim or fly? Then count the animals in the groups. Put >, <, or = in each box to compare the two groups.

Home Activity: Your child used the symbols >, <, and = to compare groups of animals. Ask your child to tell what the symbols mean and explain how he or she decided which symbol to use to compare the groups of animals.

© Pearson Education, Inc.

Notes

Family Science Activity

Camouflage

Materials
- colored paper, ripped into small pieces

Steps
1. Scatter the colored pieces of paper on the floor of your child's bedroom.
2. Have your child look and tell you which colors are the hardest to see. The hardest ones to find will be the ones that are the same color as the floor.
3. Repeat the activity in a room with a different color floor, or outside.
4. Talk with your child what this activity shows about camouflage. Camouflage is when things are colored or shaped to blend into their backgrounds or environments.
5. Ask your child to name any plants or animals he or she knows about that use camouflage.

© Pearson Education, Inc.

Take Home Booklet

Use with Chapter 3

Dear Family,

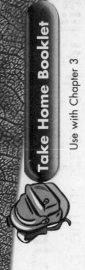

In the science chapter How Plants and Animals Live, our class is learning about different parts animals and plants have that help them live in their environments. Our class has also explored how different animals get food. The children have also learned how animals and plants protect themselves from danger.

In addition to learning how animals and plants live, the children have learned many new vocabulary words. Help your child to make these words a part of his or her own vocabulary by using them when you talk together about animals and plants.

antennae
camouflage
root
stem
flower
leaf

These following pages include activities that you and your child can do together. By participating in your child's education, you will help to bring the learning home.

Animal Body Parts

Fill in the words in the puzzle.
Use the words from the word box.

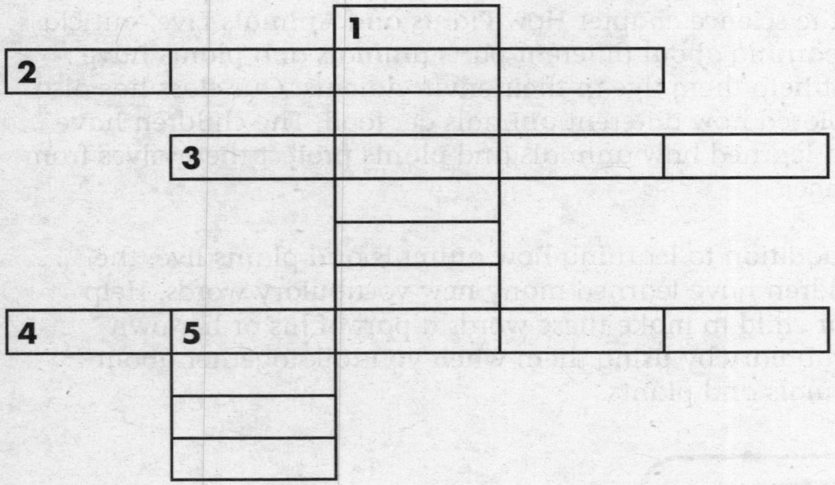

ACROSS

2 A clownfish uses these to swim in the ocean.
3 Birds break seeds or tear meat with this body part.
4 A safe, hard place where a hermit crab can live.

DOWN

1 Feelers that a crab can use to feel, smell, and taste.
5 A camel stores fat in this body part.

hump
antennae
fins
shell
beak

© Pearson Education, Inc.

Plant Parts

Look at the picture of the plant.
Label each part of the plant using a word from the box.

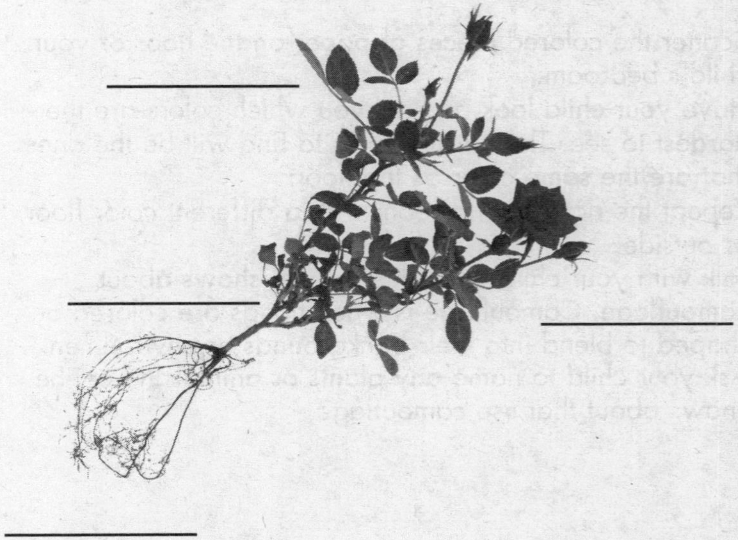

roots
stem
leaf
flower

Name ______________________________

Use with Chapter 4.

Draw a picture or write a sentence to go with each word.

life cycle	pupa
tadpole	seed coat
larva	seedling

© Pearson Education, Inc.

Directions: Read the words and draw pictures to illustrate them or write sentences about them. Cut out the boxes to use as word cards.
Home Activity: Review the vocabulary words with your child. Ask your child to choose the word or words that go with the life cycles of a frog *(tadpole)*, butterfly *(larva, pupa)*, and plant *(seed coat, seedling)*.

Name ______________________________

Use with Chapter 4.

Put Things in Order

Look at the pictures.

© Pearson Education, Inc.

Name ______________________________

Use with Chapter 4.

Apply It!

Draw pictures to show what happens first, next, and last.

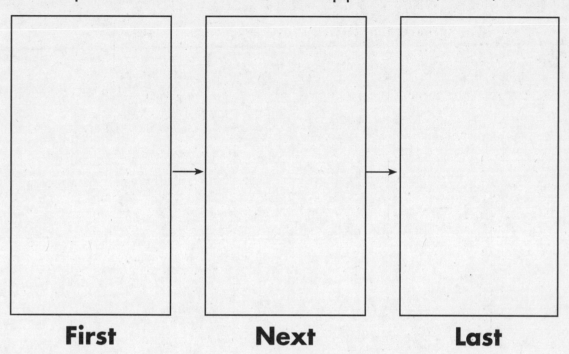

First → **Next** → **Last**

Directions: Talk about how you would put the pictures in order. Decide whether the seed, seedling, or plant is first, next, or last. Then draw pictures in the boxes to show the order.

Home Activity: Your child learned about the concept of sequence, or putting things in the order in which they happen. Point to each picture on page 34 and ask your child to tell how he or she decided whether that picture showed what happens first, next, or last.

© Pearson Education, Inc.

Notes

Name ______________________________

Use with pages 87–91.

How does a frog grow?

Before You Read Lesson 1

Read each sentence. Do you think it is true? Do you think it is not true? Circle the word or words after each sentence that tell what you think.

1. A frog begins as a tadpole.	True	Not True
2. A tadpole grows front and back legs.	True	Not True
3. A tadpole changes into a young frog.	True	Not True

After You Read Lesson 1

Read each sentence again. Circle the word or words after each sentence that tell what you think now. Did you change any answers? Put an **X** by each answer that you changed.

1. A frog begins as a tadpole.	True	Not True
2. A tadpole grows front and back legs.	True	Not True
3. A tadpole changes into a young frog.	True	Not True

© Pearson Education, Inc.

Home Activity: Together talk about your child's answers. Have your child explain why his or her answers may have changed after reading the lesson.

Name ______________________________

Use with pages 87–91.

Complete the Sentence

Write the word or phrase that completes each sentence.

hatches	life cycle	grow	tadpole

1. A frog ______________ from an egg.

2. A baby frog is called a ______________.

3. Frogs can ______________.

4. The ______________ of a frog shows how it changes.

Put Things in Order

5. Draw the parts of a frog's life cycle that are missing.

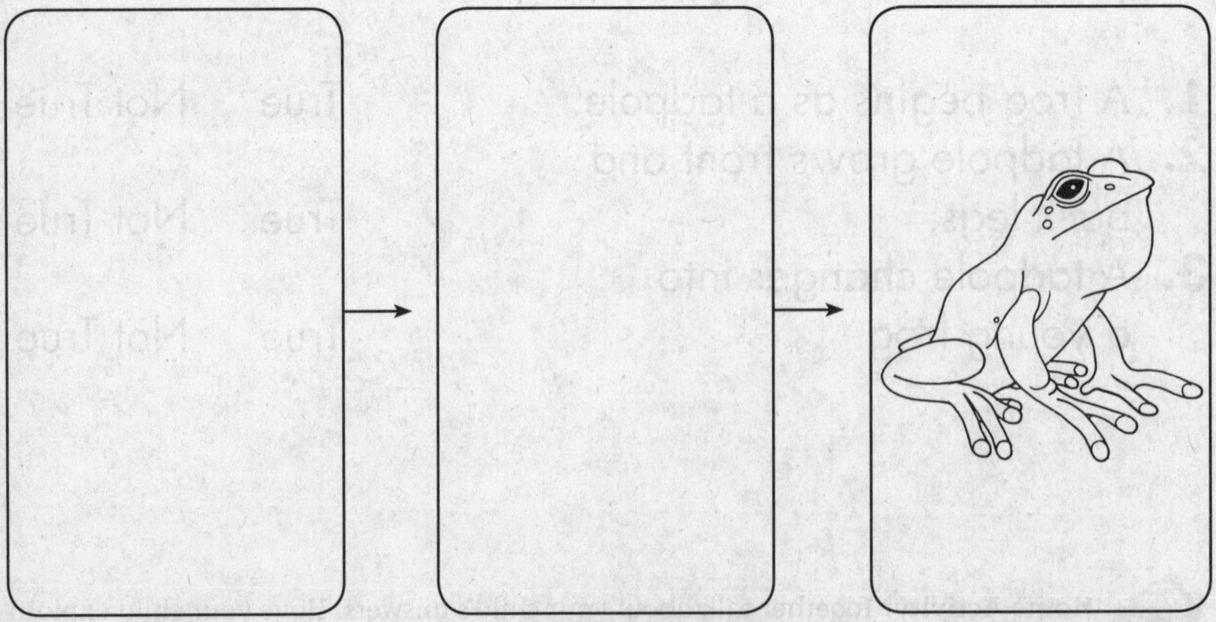

Egg **Tadpole** **Frog**

© Scott Foresman

Name ______________________________

Use with pages 92–93.

How does a butterfly grow?

Before You Read Lesson 2

Read each sentence. Do you think it is true? Do you think it is not true? Circle the word or words after each sentence that tell what you think.

1.	A butterfly begins as an egg.	True	Not True
2.	A pupa is a caterpillar.	True	Not True
3.	A butterfly flies out of the pupa.	True	Not True

After You Read Lesson 2

Read each sentence again. Circle the word or words after each sentence that tell what you think now. Did you change any answers? Put an **X** by each answer that you changed.

1.	A butterfly begins as an egg.	True	Not True
2.	A pupa is a caterpillar.	True	Not True
3.	A butterfly flies out of the pupa.	True	Not True

© Pearson Education, Inc.

Home Activity: Together talk about your child's answers. Have your child explain why his or her answers may have changed after reading the lesson.

Name ______________________

Use with pages 92–93.

Complete the Sentence

Write the word that completes each sentence.

pupa	egg	larva	changes

1. First, a butterfly is an __________.

2. When it hatches, a butterfly is a __________, or caterpillar.

3. When a butterfly is in a hard covering, it is a __________.

4. Inside the covering the butterfly __________.

Alike and Different

5. Write how a butterfly and a caterpillar are alike and different.

has wings   has antennae   has a long body

Butterfly	**Caterpiller**
	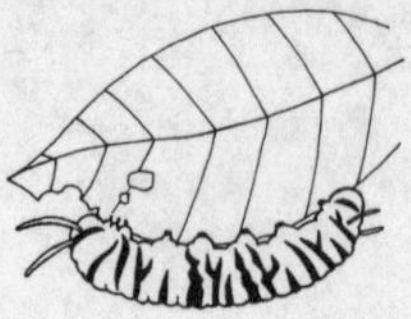

© Scott Foresman

Name ______________________________

Use with pages 94–97.

How do animals grow and change?

Before You Read Lesson 3

Read each sentence. Do you think it is true? Do you think it is not true? Circle the word or words after each sentence that tell what you think.

1.	Young animals change shape as they grow.	True	Not True
2.	Young animals change size.	True	Not True
3.	Young animals will look the same as their parents.	True	Not True

After You Read Lesson 3

Read each sentence again. Circle the word or words after each sentence that tell what you think now. Did you change any answers? Put an **X** by each answer that you changed.

1.	Young animals change shape as they grow.	True	Not True
2.	Young animals change size.	True	Not True
3.	Young animals will look the same as their parents.	True	Not True

© Pearson Education, Inc.

Home Activity: Together talk about your child's answers. Have your child explain why his or her answers may have changed after reading the lesson.

Name ____________________

Use with pages 94–97.

Complete the Sentence

Write the word that completes each sentence.

change	parents	kitten	size

1. Young animals ____________ as they grow.

2. A baby animal is not the same ____________ as an adult animal.

3. Some young animals will look like their ____________.

4. A young cat is called a ____________.

Predict

5. Predict and draw what the puppy will look like when it grows up.

I know	I predict

© Scott Foresman

Name ______________________

Use with pages 98–99.

How does a daisy grow?

Before You Read Lesson 4

Read each sentence. Do you think it is true? Do you think it is not true? Circle the word or words after each sentence that tell what you think.

1.	A seedling covers and protects a seed.	True	Not True
2.	A seedling grows from a seed.	True	Not True
3.	Flowers make seeds.	True	Not True

After You Read Lesson 4

Read each sentence again. Circle the word or words after each sentence that tell what you think now. Did you change any answers? Put an **X** by each answer that you changed.

1.	A seedling covers and protects a seed.	True	Not True
2.	A seedling grows from a seed.	True	Not True
3.	Flowers make seeds.	True	Not True

© Pearson Education, Inc.

Home Activity: Together talk about your child's answers. Have your child explain why his or her answers may have changed after reading the lesson.

Name ______________________________

Use with pages 98–99.

Complete the Sentence

Write the word or phrase that completes each sentence.

grow	seedling	roots	seed coat

1. A plant will ______________ from a seed.

2. A seed has a ______________ that keeps the seed safe.

3. When a plant is young it is called a ______________.

4. A seedling has ______________ and a stem.

Put Things in Order

5. Put the life cycle of a plant in the right order. Write "first," "next," or "last" under the pictures.

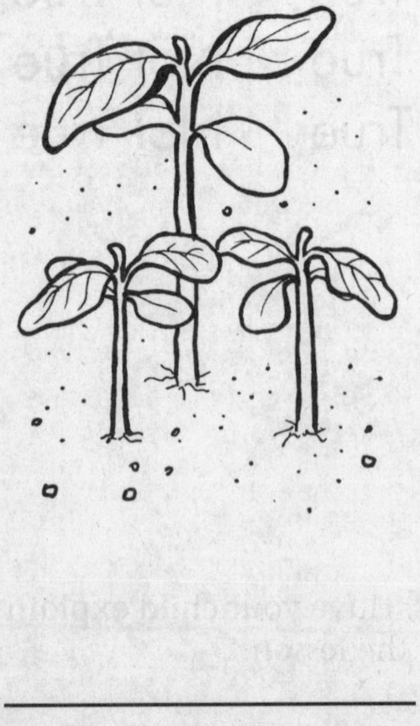

______________ ______________ ______________

© Scott Foresman

Name ______________________

Use with pages 100–103.

How do trees grow?

Before You Read Lesson 5

Read each sentence. Do you think it is true? Do you think it is not true? Circle the word or words after each sentence that tell what you think.

1. A tree grows from a seed.	True	Not True
2. Pinecones make seeds.	True	Not True
3. Cherry trees have cherries before they have flowers.	True	Not True

After You Read Lesson 5

Read each sentence again. Circle the word or words after each sentence that tell what you think now. Did you change any answers? Put an **X** by each answer that you changed.

1. A tree grows from a seed.	True	Not True
2. Pinecones make seeds.	True	Not True
3. Cherry trees have cherries before they have flowers.	True	Not True

© Pearson Education, Inc.

Home Activity: Together talk about your child's answers. Have your child explain why his or her answers may have changed after reading the lesson.

Name ______________________________

Use with pages 100–103.

Complete the Sentence

Write the word that completes each sentence.

pinecones	flowers	fruit	seeds

1. Trees grow from ______________.

2. A pine tree's seeds grow in ______________.

3. A tree can have ______________.

4. Cherry trees have ______________.

Predict

5. Predict and draw what will happen to the flowers on the tree.

I know	I predict

© Scott Foresman

Name ______________________________

Use with pages 104–105.

How do plants grow and change?

Before You Read Lesson 6

Read each sentence. Do you think it is true? Do you think it is not true? Circle the word or words after each sentence that tell what you think.

1.	Young plants change as they grow.	True	Not True
2.	Tulips have different color patterns.	True	Not True
3.	An oak seedling and an oak tree both have big leaves.	True	Not True

After You Read Lesson 6

Read each sentence again. Circle the word or words after each sentence that tell what you think now. Did you change any answers? Put an **X** by each answer that you changed.

1.	Young plants change as they grow.	True	Not True
2.	Tulips have different color patterns.	True	Not True
3.	An oak seedling and an oak tree both have big leaves.	True	Not True

© Pearson Education, Inc.

Home Activity: Together talk about your child's answers. Have your child explain why his or her answers may have changed after reading the lesson.

Name ______________________________

Use with pages 104–105.

Complete the Sentence

Write the word that completes each sentence.

stem	colors	grow	petals

1. Flowers can be many different ____________.

2. A rose's ______________ look different than a tulip's.

3. When an oak tree is a seedling, it has a thin ________________.

4. An oak tree will ____________ into a big tree.

Alike and Different

5. Write one way the flowers are alike and one way they are different.

Alike: ____________________________

Different: ____________________________

____

© Scott Foresman

Name ______________________________

Use with Chapter 4.

Comparing Size and Age

Look at the pictures of the tree.
Fill in the chart.

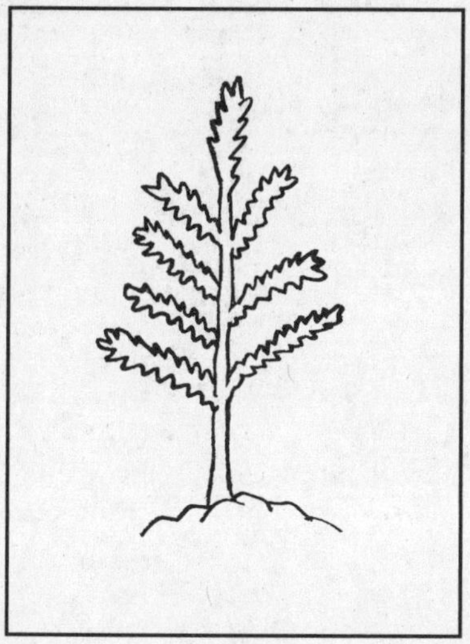

The tree is two years old. It is 4 feet tall.

The tree is five years old. It is 10 feet tall.

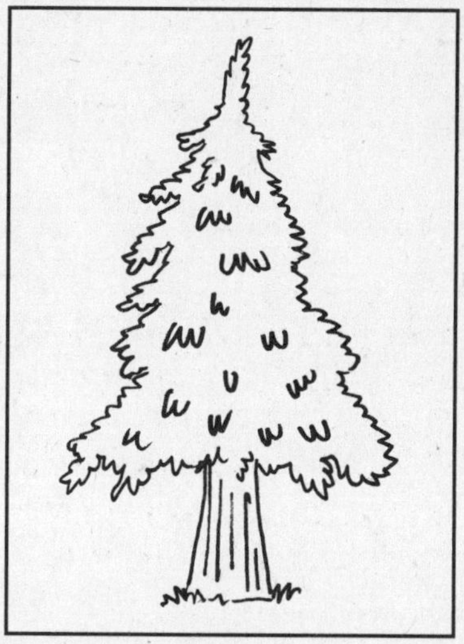

The tree is ten years old. It is 20 feet tall.

Age	Size
____ years old	____ feet tall
____ years old	____ feet tall
____ years old	____ feet tall

© Pearson Education, Inc.

Directions: Look at the pictures and read the captions. Use the information to fill in the blanks in the chart.
Home Activity: Your child learned how to fill in a chart to compare size and age. Ask your child questions about the information in the chart, such as *How tall was the tree when it was two years old? How much taller was the tree at ten years than at five years?*

Notes

Family Science Activity
Plant Life Cycle

Materials
- plastic cup
- paper towels
- 1 bean
- plastic wrap
- paper
- pencil

Steps
1. Dampen 1 or 2 paper towels and lay them in the bottom of the plastic cup.
2. Place a bean on the paper towel in the cup. Try to place the bean in a fold of the paper towel so it does not move around. Place a small piece of plastic wrap over the top of the cup.
3. Have your child draw a picture of the bean in the cup.
4. Every day have your child moisten the paper towel so it is damp, not soaking wet. Then, have your child draw a picture of any changes in the bean.
5. The seed coat of the bean should open after about three days and the seedling will begin to grow. Encourage your child to continue to observe and draw the growth of the bean plant.

© Pearson Education, Inc.

Dear Family,

Your child is learning about how animals and plants change as they grow. In the science chapter Life Cycles, our class has studied the life cycles of frogs and butterflies. We have also learned how other animals change as they grow. The children have also learned that different types of plants have different life cycles.

In addition to learning how to animals and plants change as they grow, the children have also learned many new vocabulary words. Help your child to make these words a part of his or her own vocabulary by using them when you talk together about life cycles.

tadpole
life cycle
larva
pupa
seed coat
seedling

These following pages include activities that you and your child can do together. By participating in your child's education, you will help to bring the learning home.

Circle the words in the puzzle.

tadpole	pupa	seed coat
larva	seedling	life cycle

T	S	E	E	D	C	O	A	T	R
A	R	V	V	N	E	S	P	J	L
D	W	Z	R	P	D	P	O	L	I
P	U	P	A	U	L	S	E	D	F
O	O	W	F	P	B	R	E	D	E
L	A	R	V	A	S	O	L	A	C
E	S	K	P	M	E	E	A	D	Y
Q	M	J	E	A	I	G	R	T	C
U	S	E	E	D	L	I	N	G	L
P	A	T	T	E	F	U	O	M	E

Fun Fact

Redwood trees are some of the tallest and biggest trees in the world. They are also some of the oldest trees.
Many of these trees live to be about 600 years old. But some redwood trees have been alive for over 2,000 years!

© Pearson Education, Inc.

Literacy and Art

Look at the life cycle of the butterfly.
Label each part of the life cycle using a word from the box.

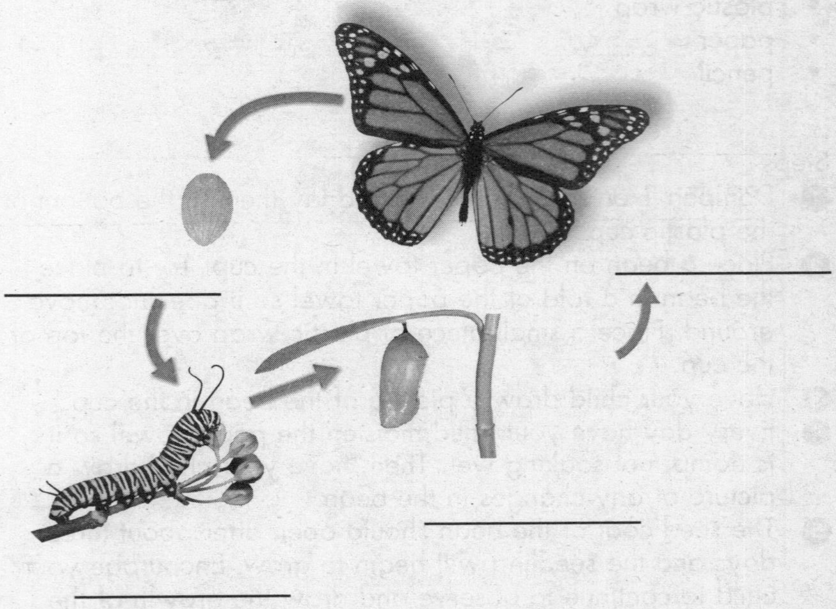

egg
pupa
butterfly
larva

Name ____________________

Vocabulary Preview

Use with Chapter 5.

Draw a picture or write a sentence to go with each word.

food chain	rain forest
oxygen	marsh

Directions: Read the words and draw pictures to illustrate them or write sentences about them. Cut out the boxes to use as word cards.
Home Activity: Review the vocabulary words with your child. Ask your child to use each word in a sentence that tells about the word.

© Pearson Education, Inc.

Name ______________________

How to Read Science

Use with Chapter 5.

Draw Conclusions

Look at the picture.
Write your answer in the boxes.

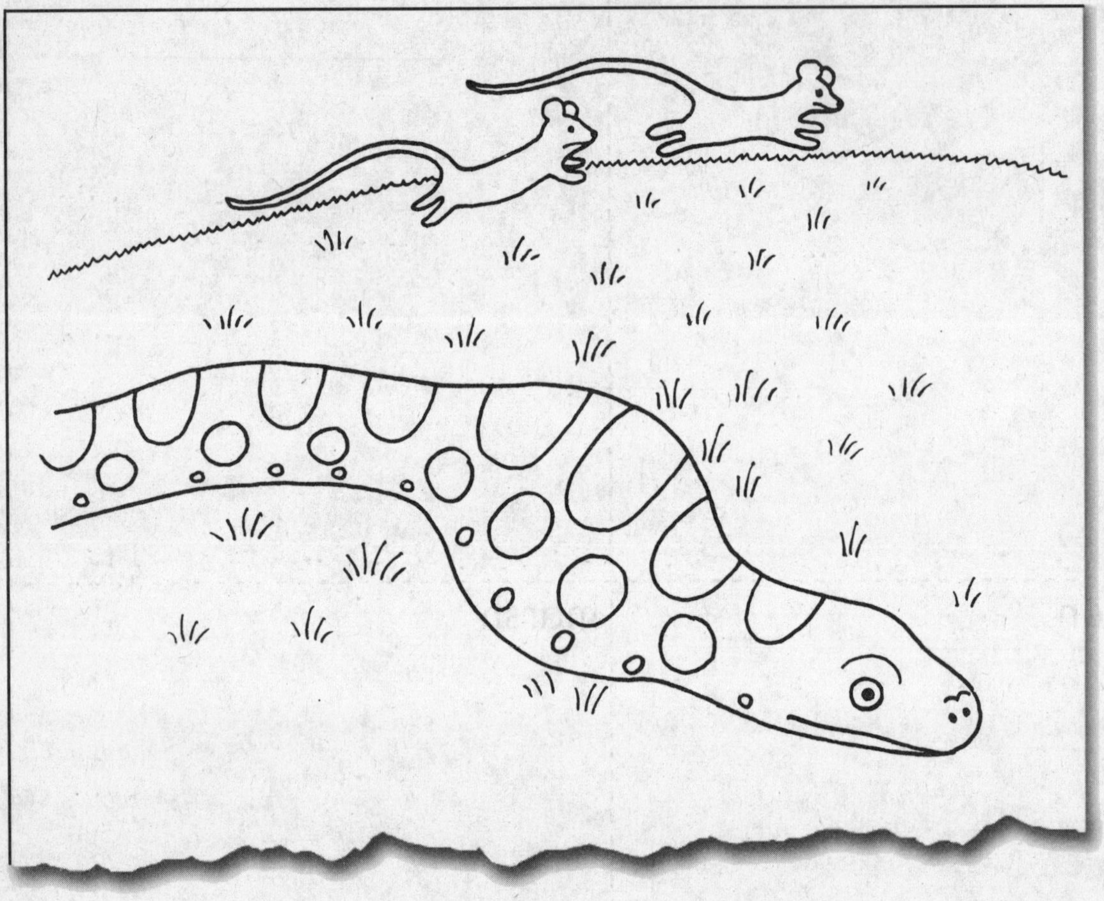

© Pearson Education, Inc.

Name ______________________________

Use with Chapter 5.

Apply It!

Infer: What do you think the snake did?

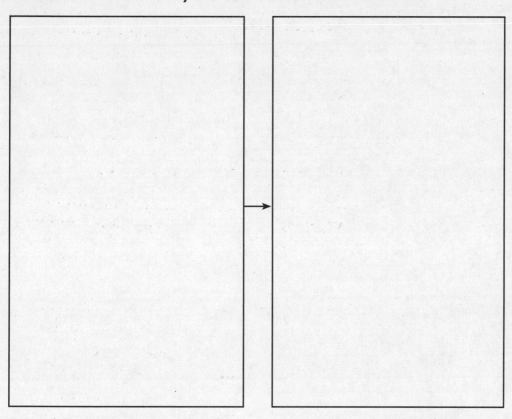

I know	→	My conclusion

© Pearson Education, Inc.

Directions: Look closely at the picture. What do you think the snake has done? Draw a conclusion about what you see. Tell what you know. Tell your conclusion.
Home Activity: Your child learned about drawing conclusions. Show your child a picture in a magazine or newspaper, but cover the caption. Ask your child to tell what he or she thinks is happening in the picture and why. Then read the caption aloud.

Notes

Name ______________________

Use with pages 119–121.

How do plants and animals get food?

Before You Read Lesson 1

Read each sentence. Do you think it is true? Do you think it is not true? Circle the word or words after each sentence that tell what you think.

1.	Green plants can make their own food.	True	Not True
2.	All animals eat plants.	True	Not True
3.	Some animals eat other animals.	True	Not True

After You Read Lesson 1

Read each sentence again. Circle the word or words after each sentence that tell what you think now. Did you change any answers? Put an **X** by each answer that you changed.

1.	Green plants can make their own food.	True	Not True
2.	All animals eat plants.	True	Not True
3.	Some animals eat other animals.	True	Not True

© Pearson Education, Inc.

Home Activity: Together talk about your child's answers. Have your child explain why his or her answers may have changed after reading the lesson.

Name ______________________________

Use with pages 119–121.

Complete the Sentence

Write the word that completes each sentence.
Use each word twice.

oxygen	food

1. Animals eat different kinds of ____________.

2. A plant makes its own ____________.

3. Animals use ______________ to help them live.

4. Green leaves give off ____________ when they make food.

Draw Conclusions

5. Write what the bird is going to do with the worm.

© Scott Foresman

Name ________________________________

Use with pages 122–125.

How do living things get food in a rain forest?

Before You Read Lesson 2

Read each sentence. Do you think it is true? Do you think it is not true? Circle the word or words after each sentence that tell what you think.

1.	Plants are food for insects.	True	Not True
2.	Insects are food for other animals.	True	Not True
3.	Plants are not part of any food chain.	True	Not True

After You Read Lesson 2

Read each sentence again. Circle the word or words after each sentence that tell what you think now. Did you change any answers? Put an **X** by each answer that you changed.

1.	Plants are food for insects.	True	Not True
2.	Insects are food for other animals.	True	Not True
3.	Plants are not part of any food chain.	True	Not True

Home Activity: Together talk about your child's answers. Have your child explain why his or her answers may have changed after reading the lesson.

© Pearson Education, Inc.

Name ______________________

Use with pages 122–125.

Complete the Sentence

Write the word or phrase that completes each sentence.

food chain	grow	food	rain forest

1. A bird eating a worm is part of a ____________.

2. A ____________ is a habitat.

3. The plants in the habitat make ____________.

4. Many plants ____________ in this habitat.

Predict

5. Predict and color the plant or animal that the giraffe will eat.

Giraffe	Living Things

© Scott Foresman

Name ______________________________

Use with pages 126–129.

How do living things get food in a marsh?

Before You Read Lesson 3

Read each sentence. Do you think it is true? Do you think it is not true? Circle the word or words after each sentence that tell what you think.

1. A food chain does not begin with plants.	True	Not True
2. Animals are food for other animals.	True	Not True
3. A marsh is a wetland habitat.	True	Not True

After You Read Lesson 3

Read each sentence again. Circle the word or words after each sentence that tell what you think now. Did you change any answers? Put an **X** by each answer that you changed.

1. A food chain does not begin with plants.	True	Not True
2. Animals are food for other animals.	True	Not True
3. A marsh is a wetland habitat.	True	Not True

© Pearson Education, Inc.

Home Activity: Together talk about your child's answers. Have your child explain why his or her answers may have changed after reading the lesson.

Name ______________________________

Lesson 3 Review

Use with pages 126–129.

Complete the Sentence

Write the word or phrase that completes each sentence.

eat	food chain	marsh	sunlight

1. A ____________ is a wetland habitat.

2. This habitat has a ____________.

3. Some animals ____________ plants and other animals.

4. Plants use ____________ to make food.

Predict

5. Predict and write what will happen between the animals.

© Scott Foresman

Name ______________________________

Use with Chapter 5.

Grouping Animals

Read the sentences.
Fill in the Venn diagram with the names of the animals.

A **bear** eats plants and animals.

A **snake** eats only other animals.

A **snail** eats only plants.

An **eagle** eats only other animals.

A **mouse** eats only plants.

Grouping Animals by What They Eat

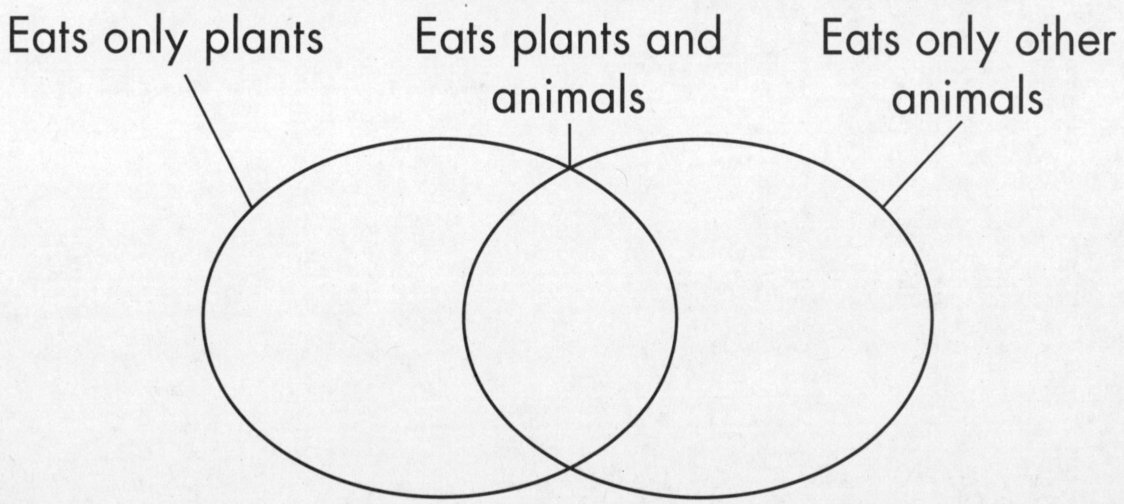

Directions: Read each sentence. Think about what the animal eats. Decide where the animal fits in the Venn diagram. Write the animal's name in the correct place.
Home Activity: Your child learned how to use a Venn diagram. Ask your child to explain how he or she filled in the Venn diagram. Then together make your own Venn diagram showing, for example, animals you like, animals your child likes, and animals you both like.

© Pearson Education, Inc.

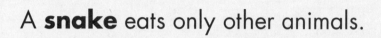

Notes

Family Science Activity

Food Chains in Your Neighborhood

Materials
- 10 index cards
- crayons

Steps
1. Take your child on a walk around the neighborhood. Have your child identify 10 living things on your walk.
2. On the index cards, have your child draw a picture of each of the living things.
3. Talk with your child about a way that the living things can form a food chain. Have your child arrange the cards in a food chain. Your child may not use all of his or her cards. Encourage your child to try to make a chain of four cards.
4. Ask your child if he or she can tell you ways the food chain he or she made is the same or different from the rain forest food chain and the marsh food chain.

© Pearson Education, Inc.

Take Home Booklet

Use with Chapter 5

Dear Family,

In the science chapter Food Chains, our class is learning how plants and animals get food. Our class explored how plants use water, sunlight, and air to make their own food. The children have also learned about food chains in the rain forest and in the marsh.

In addition to learning about food chains, the children have also learned many new vocabulary words. Help your child to make these words a part of his or her own vocabulary by using them when you talk together about food chains.

oxygen
rain forest
food chain
marsh

These following pages include activities that you and your child can do together. By participating in your child's education, you will help to bring the learning home.

Marsh Food Chain

Look at the pictures.
Draw lines from the pictures to the place the picture belongs in the food chain. The first line has been drawn for you.

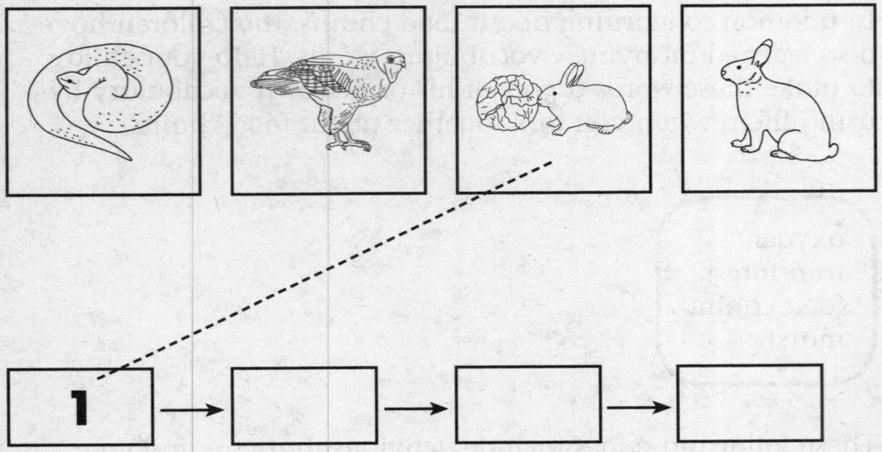

© Pearson Education, Inc.

Plants Make Food

Color the plant
Circle the three things the plant needs to make food.

air

insects

sunlight

water

snow

Name ______________________________

Use with Chapter 6.

Draw a picture or write a sentence to go with each word.

sand	rocks
clay	weathering
humus	erosion
natural resource	minerals

© Pearson Education, Inc.

Directions: Read the words and draw pictures to illustrate them or write sentences about them. Cut out the boxes to use as word cards.
Home Activity: Review the vocabulary words with your child. Read aloud the meaning of one of the words from the glossary in your child's textbook. Have your child name the word that goes with the definition.

Name ____________________

Use with Chapter 6.

Important Details

Look at the picture.
Read the sentences.
Look for important details.

Science Diagram

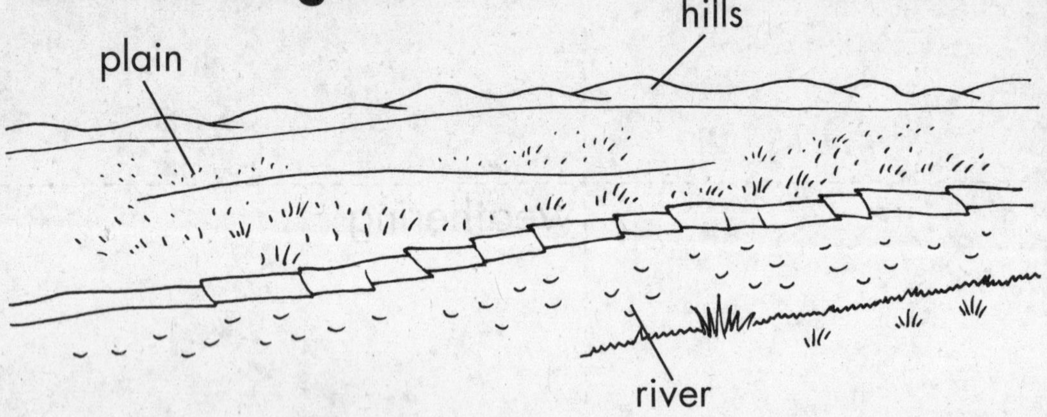

This place has two kinds of land.
It has a plain and hills.
This place has one kind of water.
It has a river.

© Pearson Education, Inc.

Name ______________________________

Apply It!

Suppose you are going to make a model of this place. What important details would you show?

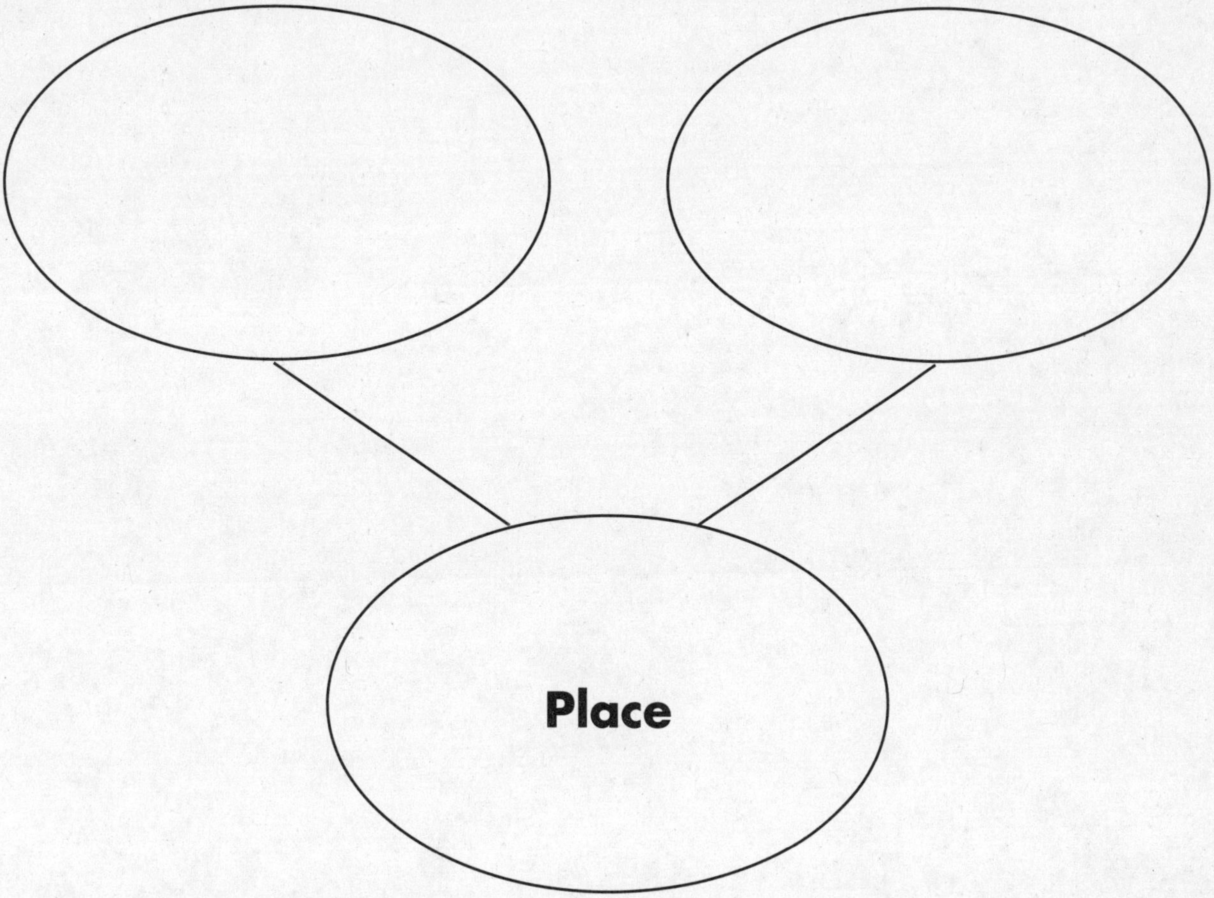

© Pearson Education, Inc.

Directions: As you look at the picture and read the sentences, think about the important details. Ask yourself which details in the picture and words tell you something. Then answer the question.

Home Activity: Your child learned about recognizing important details in pictures and words. Review the important details on the page. Then together look at a magazine or newspaper picture and decide what you think are important details in the picture.

Notes

Name ________________________________

Use with pages 151–153.

What makes up Earth?

Before You Read Lesson 1

Read each sentence. Do you think it is true? Do you think it is not true? Circle the word or words after each sentence that tell what you think.

1.	Earth has more land than water.	True	Not True
2.	A plain is flat land.	True	Not True
3.	A cliff is steep land.	True	Not True

After You Read Lesson 1

Read each sentence again. Circle the word or words after each sentence that tell what you think now. Did you change any answers? Put an **X** by each answer that you changed.

1.	Earth has more land than water.	True	Not True
2.	A plain is flat land.	True	Not True
3.	A cliff is steep land.	True	Not True

© Pearson Education, Inc.

Home Activity: Together talk about your child's answers. Have your child explain why his or her answers may have changed after reading the lesson.

Name ______________________

Use with pages 151–153.

Complete the Sentence

Write the word that completes each sentence.

land	plain	cliff	lake

1. Part of Earth is made of __________.

2. A ______________ is filled with water.

3. A ______________ is part of Earth that is flat.

4. A ______________ is land that is very steep.

Alike and Different

5. Write how a river and a lake are alike and different.

River	Lake

© Scott Foresman

Name ______________________

Think, Read, Learn

Use with pages 154–157.

What are rocks and soil?

Before You Read Lesson 2

Read each sentence. Do you think it is true? Do you think it is not true? Circle the word or words after each sentence that tell what you think.

1. Tiny pieces of broken rock are called sand.	True	Not True
2. Sand feels sticky and soft.	True	Not True
3. Humus helps plants grow.	True	Not True

After You Read Lesson 2

Read each sentence again. Circle the word or words after each sentence that tell what you think now. Did you change any answers? Put an **X** by each answer that you changed.

1. Tiny pieces of broken rock are called sand.	True	Not True
2. Sand feels sticky and soft.	True	Not True
3. Humus helps plants grow.	True	Not True

© Pearson Education, Inc.

Home Activity: Together talk about your child's answers. Have your child explain why his or her answers may have changed after reading the lesson.

Name ______________________________

Lesson 2 Review

Use with pages 154–157.

Complete the Sentence

Write the word or phrase that completes each sentence.

sand	natural resource	humus	clay

1. A ______________ is a part of Earth that living things use.

2. Tiny pieces of rock are called ______________.

3. Most plants cannot grow in ______________ soil.

4. Soil may have sand, clay, and ______________ in it.

Important Details

5. Write two important details you learned about natural resources.

Natural Resources

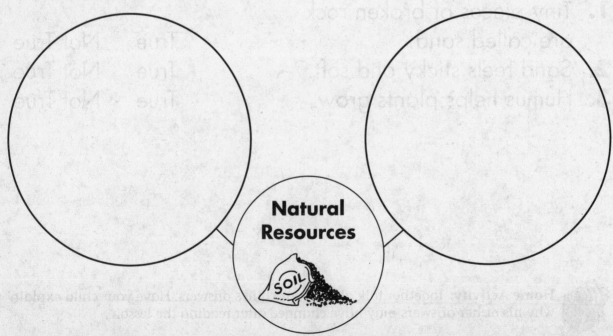

© Scott Foresman

Name ______________________________

Use with pages 158–159.

What changes land?

Before You Read Lesson 3

Read each sentence. Do you think it is true? Do you think it is not true? Circle the word or words after each sentence that tell what you think.

1. Water and ice cause weathering.	True	Not True
2. Wind and water can move rocks and soil.	True	Not True
3. Weathering happens quickly.	True	Not True

After You Read Lesson 3

Read each sentence again. Circle the word or words after each sentence that tell what you think now. Did you change any answers? Put an **X** by each answer that you changed.

1. Water and ice cause weathering.	True	Not True
2. Wind and water can move rocks and soil.	True	Not True
3. Weathering happens quickly.	True	Not True

© Pearson Education, Inc.

Home Activity: Together talk about your child's answers. Have your child explain why his or her answers may have changed after reading the lesson.

Name ____________________

Use with pages 158–159.

Complete the Sentence

Write the word that completes each sentence.

erosion	water	weathering	plants

1. Rocks change size and shape during ________.

2. Rocks and soil move during ________.

3. Wind and ________ can cause erosion.

4. Roots of ________ can help keep soil in place.

Predict

5. Predict and draw what will happen to the pile of soil.

I know	I predict

© Scott Foresman

Name ______________________

Use with pages 160–165.

How do living things use natural resources?

Before You Read Lesson 4

Read each sentence. Do you think it is true? Do you think it is not true? Circle the word or words after each sentence that tell what you think.

1. Only animals need clean air. True Not True
2. People and animals use water for drinking. True Not True
3. People get food and minerals from land. True Not True

After You Read Lesson 4

Read each sentence again. Circle the word or words after each sentence that tell what you think now. Did you change any answers? Put an **X** by each answer that you changed.

1. Only animals need clean air. True Not True
2. People and animals use water for drinking. True Not True
3. People get food and minerals from land. True Not True

© Pearson Education, Inc.

Home Activity: Together talk about your child's answers. Have your child explain why his or her answers may have changed after reading the lesson.

Name ______________________________

Use with pages 160–165.

Complete the Sentence

Write the word that completes each sentence.

mineral	air	water	land

1. A natural resource that we breathe is __________.

2. We use __________ to grow food.

3. People use __________ for drinking.

4. Gold is a __________.

Picture Clues

5. Use picture clues to write how water is being used in the pictures.

______________________________ ______________________________

______________________________ ______________________________

______________________________ ______________________________

© Scott Foresman

Use with pages 166–167.

How can you reduce, reuse, and recycle?

Before You Read Lesson 5

Read each sentence. Do you think it is true? Do you think it is not true? Circle the word or words after each sentence that tell what you think.

1. *Reduce* means to use less. True Not True
2. When you reuse, you use things more than one time. True Not True
3. You cannot recycle a milk carton. True Not True

After You Read Lesson 5

Read each sentence again. Circle the word or words after each sentence that tell what you think now. Did you change any answers? Put an **X** by each answer that you changed.

1. *Reduce* means to use less. True Not True
2. When you reuse, you use things more than one time. True Not True
3. You cannot recycle a milk carton. True Not True

© Pearson Education, Inc.

Home Activity: Together talk about your child's answers. Have your child explain why his or her answers may have changed after reading the lesson.

Name ______________________________

Lesson 5 Review

Use with pages 166–167.

Complete the Sentence

Write the word that completes each sentence.

reduce	resources	recycle	reuse

1. When you use less of something, you ____________.

2. When you use something again, you ____________.

3. When you take an old thing and make it new, you ____________.

4. It is good to save Earth's ____________.

Draw Conclusions

5. Write what the man in the picture is doing.

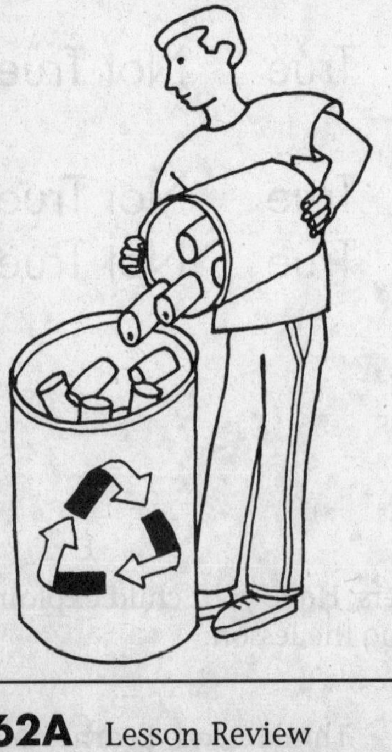

© Scott Foresman

Name ______________________________

Use with Chapter 6.

Reading a Picture Graph

Amy, Jay, and Leo collected cans to recycle. The picture graph shows how many cans they collected.

Use the picture graph to answer the questions.

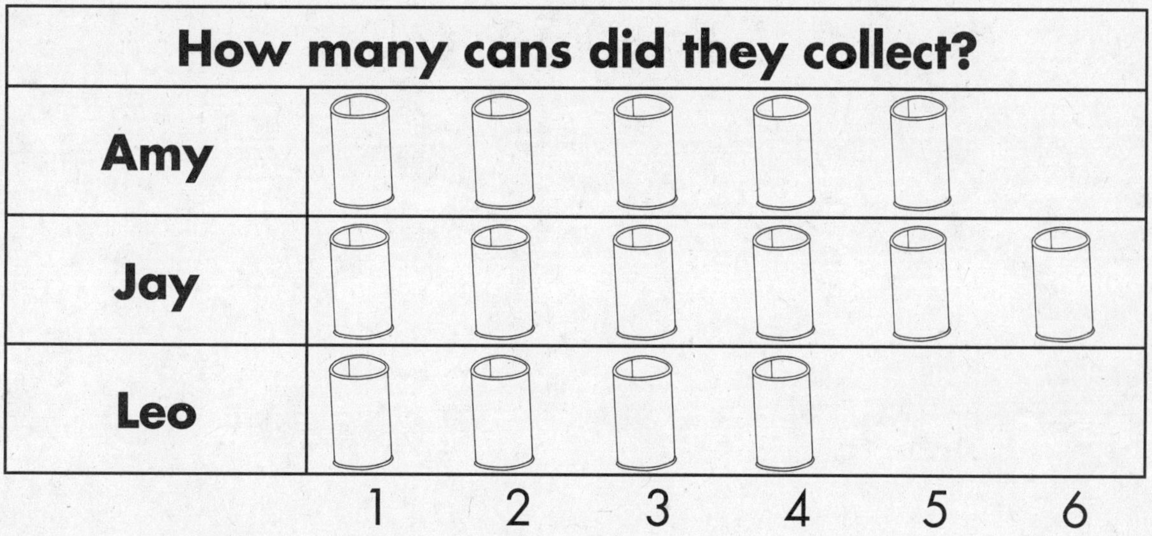

1. Did Amy or Jay collect more cans? ______________

2. How many cans did Amy, Jay, and Leo collect all together? ______________

© Pearson Education, Inc.

Directions: The picture graph shows the number of cans each child collected. Each picture of a can stands for one can collected. Count the cans in each row. Then answer the questions by subtracting or adding those numbers.
Home Activity: Your child learned how to read a picture graph. Ask your child to explain how he or she answered the questions about the graph. Then ask other questions, such as *How many more cans did Jay collect than Leo? Who collected the fewest cans?*

Notes

Family Science Activity

Set Up a Recycling Center

Materials
- paper
- crayons
- several plastic totes or cardboard boxes
- tape

Steps
1. Research with your child the materials that can be recycled in your community.
2. On paper, have your child write the names of the materials that can be recycled, such as "tin" or "clear glass."
3. Talk with your child about the kinds of materials that can go into each box. Point out that the materials to be recycled have to be clean.
4. Ask your child to think of any ways to reuse materials in the house to decrease the amount of trash and recycling.
5. Encourage your child to explain the new recycling center to others in the household. Have your child explain both how to use the center and how the center helps protect natural resources.

© Pearson Education, Inc.

Take Home Booklet

Use with Chapter 6

Dear Family,

In the science chapter Land, Water, and Air, our class is learning what makes up Earth. Our class learned how Earth is made of different kinds of land and water. The children have also learned how living things use natural resources. The children learned that there are ways to protect natural resources, including reusing, reducing, and recycling.

In addition to learning about Earth's land, water, and air, the children have also learned many new vocabulary words. Help your child to make these words a part of his or her own vocabulary by using them when you talk together about Earth's land, water, and air.

rocks
sand
natural resource
clay
humus
weathering
erosion
minerals

The following pages include activities that you and your child can do together. By participating in your child's education, you will help to bring the learning home.

Name That Soil

Read the sentences.
Fill in the missing word. Look at the choices in the box below.

clay
humus
sand

Count the number of lines for each answer. This is the number of letters in the word.

1 What kind of soil is loose and easy to dig?

___ ___ ___ ___

2 What kind of soil is made from living things that died?

___ ___ ___ ___ ___

3 What kind of soil is sticky and soft?

___ ___ ___ ___

© Pearson Education, Inc.

Kinds of Land and Water

Look at the pictures.
Draw a line from the picture to the word that describes the picture.

plain

lake

river

cliff

Name ______________________________

Vocabulary Preview

Use with Chapter 7.

Draw a picture or write a sentence to go with each word.

season	water vapor
weather	clouds
temperature	sleet
thermometer	

© Pearson Education, Inc.

Directions: Read the words and draw pictures to illustrate them or write sentences about them. Cut out the boxes to use as word cards.
Home Activity: Discuss with your child how the vocabulary words in each pair are related to each other: *season* and *weather, temperature* and *thermometer, clou*
and *water vapor.*

Name ______________________________

Use with Chapter 7.

Predict

Read the science story.
Answer the question on the next page.

Rain

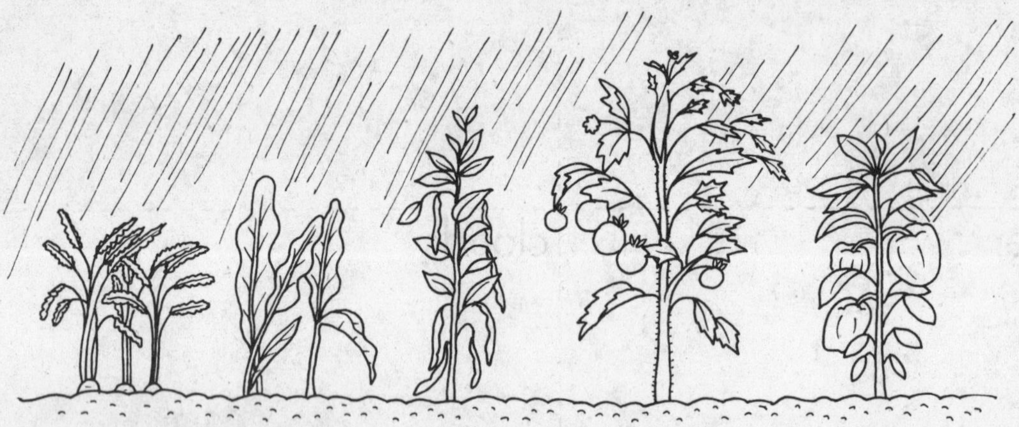

It is raining. The plants need the rain.
The rain helps the plants grow.

© Pearson Education, Inc.

Name ______________________

Use with Chapter 7.

Apply It!

Predict What will happen to the plants if it does not rain for a long time?

I know.	→	I predict.

Directions: Read the science story and look at the picture. Then read the question. Use what the story told you to make a guess about what will happen to the plants if they do not get any rain.

Home Activity: Your child learned about making predictions based on prior knowledge. Put a book on the edge of a table and ask your child what will happen if you push the book off the table. (It will fall on the floor.) Set up similar situations and ask your child to predict.

© Pearson Education, Inc.

Notes

Use with pages 183–185.

How can you measure weather?

Before You Read Lesson 1

Read each sentence. Do you think it is true? Do you think it is not true? Circle the word or words after each sentence that tell what you think.

1. Weather is what the air is like outside.	True	Not True
2. Weather may be windy or sunny.	True	Not True
3. A wind vane measures how hot or cold it is.	True	Not True

After You Read Lesson 1

Read each sentence again. Circle the word or words after each sentence that tell what you think now. Did you change any answers? Put an **X** by each answer that you changed.

1. Weather is what the air is like outside.	True	Not True
2. Weather may be windy or sunny.	True	Not True
3. A wind vane measures how hot or cold it is.	True	Not True

© Pearson Education, Inc.

Home Activity: Together talk about your child's answers. Have your child explain why his or her answers may have changed after reading the lesson.

Name ______________________

Use with pages 183–185.

Complete the Sentence

Write the word that completes each sentence.

thermometer	sunny	weather	temperature

1. A ____________ can tell how hot or cold it is outside.

2. Sometimes, the ____________ is rainy.

3. Some days are hot and ____________.

4. A ____________ is a number that tells how hot or cold something is.

Picture Clues

5. Use picture clues to tell what the weather is like in the picture.

© Scott Foresman

Name ______________________________

Use with pages 186–187.

How do clouds form?

Before You Read Lesson 2

Read each sentence. Do you think it is true? Do you think it is not true? Circle the word or words after each sentence that tell what you think.

1.	You can see water vapor.	True	Not True
2.	Fluffy clouds mean good weather.	True	Not True
3.	Fog is a cloud near the ground.	True	Not True

After You Read Lesson 2

Read each sentence again. Circle the word or words after each sentence that tell what you think now. Did you change any answers? Put an **X** by each answer that you changed.

1.	You can see water vapor.	True	Not True
2.	Fluffy clouds mean good weather.	True	Not True
3.	Fog is a cloud near the ground.	True	Not True

© Pearson Education, Inc.

Home Activity: Together talk about your child's answers. Have your child explain why his or her answers may have changed after reading the lesson.

Name ______________________________

Lesson 2 Review

Use with pages 186–187.

Complete the Sentence

Write the word or phrase that completes each sentence.

water vapor	weather	clouds	rain

1. A form of water in the air is called __________.

2. Tiny drops of water in the sky form __________.

3. If you look at the sky you can tell what the __________ will be like.

4. A gray sky means it might __________.

Predict

5. Predict and draw what will happen in the picture.

I know	I predict

© Scott Foresman

Name ____________________

Use with pages 188–191.

What are some kinds of wet weather?

Before You Read Lesson 3

Read each sentence. Do you think it is true? Do you think it is not true? Circle the word or words after each sentence that tell what you think.

1.	Many animals look for shelter when it rains.	True	Not True
2.	Sleet falls when it is warm.	True	Not True
3.	Snow falls in cold weather.	True	Not True

After You Read Lesson 3

Read each sentence again. Circle the word or words after each sentence that tell what you think now. Did you change any answers? Put an **X** by each answer that you changed.

1.	Many animals look for shelter when it rains.	True	Not True
2.	Sleet falls when it is warm.	True	Not True
3.	Snow falls in cold weather.	True	Not True

© Pearson Education, Inc.

Home Activity: Together talk about your child's answers. Have your child explain why his or her answers may have changed after reading the lesson.

Name ______________________________

Use with pages 188–191.

Complete the Sentence

Write the word that completes each sentence.

shelter	snow	sleet	wet

1. A rainy day is ______________ weather.

2. Frozen rain is ______________.

3. On rainy days animals and people want ______________.

4. Water that freezes high in the air is ______________.

Alike and Different

5. Write how the kinds of weather below are alike or different.

Rainy Day	**Sunny Day**
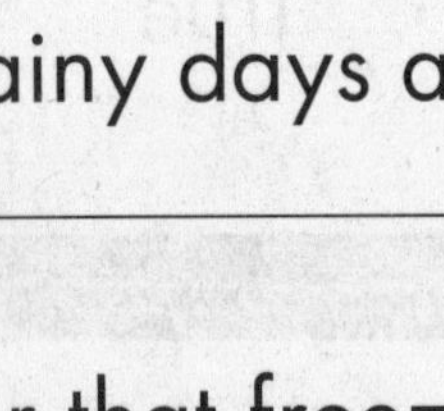	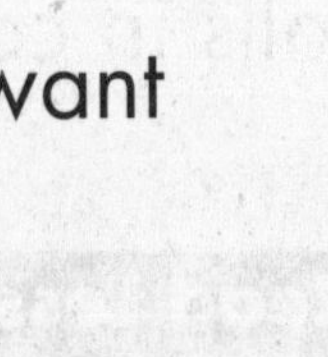

© Scott Foresman

Name ______________________________

Use with pages 192–193.

What are the four seasons?

Before You Read Lesson 4

Read each sentence. Do you think it is true? Do you think it is not true? Circle the word or words after each sentence that tell what you think.

1. Summer comes after spring. True Not True
2. Spring and summer are warm seasons. True Not True
3. Fall comes after winter. True Not True

After You Read Lesson 4

Read each sentence again. Circle the word or words after each sentence that tell what you think now. Did you change any answers? Put an **X** by each answer that you changed.

1. Summer comes after spring. True Not True
2. Spring and summer are warm seasons. True Not True
3. Fall comes after winter. True Not True

© Pearson Education, Inc.

Home Activity: Together talk about your child's answers. Have your child explain why his or her answers may have changed after reading the lesson.

Name ____________________

Use with pages 192–193.

Complete the Sentence

Write the word that completes each sentence.

spring	fall	summer	season

1. It rains a lot in the __________.

2. It is very hot in the __________.

3. Leaves change color in the __________.

4. Winter is a __________, or a time of year.

Draw Conclusions

5. Write what seasons are shown in the pictures below. Write spring, summer, winter, or fall.

__________ __________

© Scott Foresman

Name ______________________________ **Math** in Science

Use with Chapter 7

Using a Bar Graph

Anchorage, Alaska, gets about 110 cm of snow in the winter.

How much snow falls in Anchorage, Alaska in the winter?

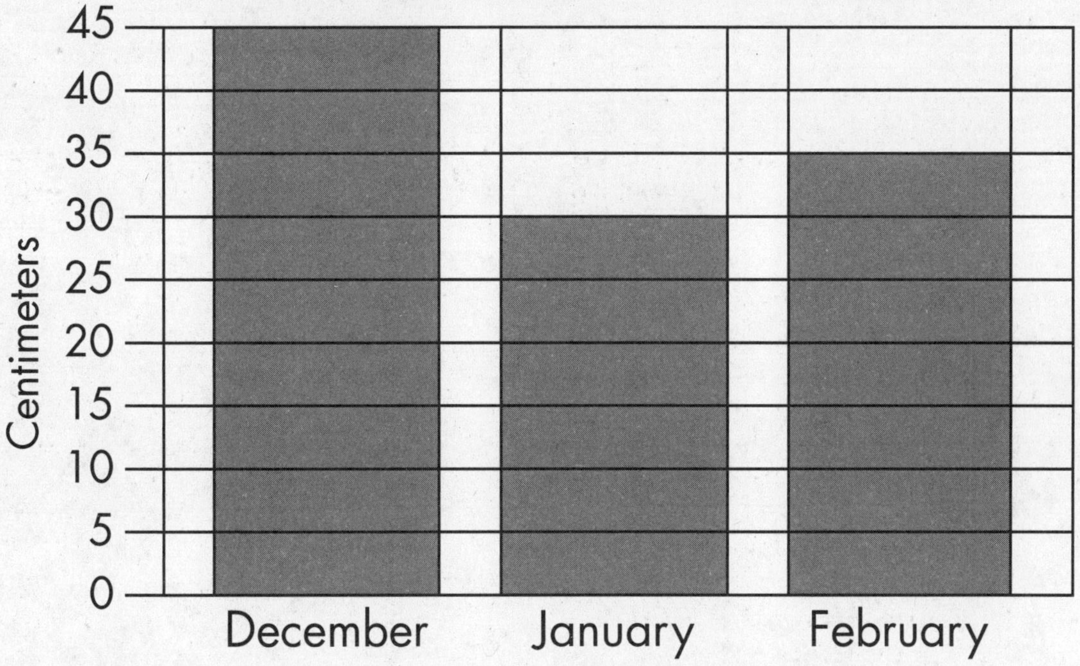

Use the bar graph to answer these questions.

1. Which month gets the most snow in Anchorage? ____________

2. Which month gets the least snow in Anchorage? ____________

3. How much more snow does Anchorage get in December than in February? ____________

© Pearson Education, Inc.

Directions: The bar graph shows how much snow the city of Anchorage, Alaska gets in three winter months, December, January, and February. To find the amount of snow for a month, trace the line at the top of the bar to the number at the left. Use the numbers to answer the questions.
Home Activity: Your child learned how to use a bar graph. Ask your child other questions about the graph, such as *Does Anchorage get more snow in January or February? How much snow does Anchorage get altogether in the winter?*

Notes

Family Science Activity

Make Your Own Rain

Materials

- glass jar, such as a mayonnaise jar
- plate
- ice cubes
- hot water

Steps

1. Place two to three inches of very warm tap water into the glass jar. (An adult should do this.)
2. Cover the lid of the jar with a small plate and let it sit for 2 – 3 minutes.
3. Then have your child carefully place two or three ice cubes on top of the plate.
4. Observe what happens inside the jar with your child. Inside the jar it should look like it is raining.
5. Ask your child to name the type of wet weather. Encourage your child to identify other types of wet weather he or she knows.

© Pearson Education, Inc.

Dear Family,

In the science chapter Weather, your child is learning about different types of weather and tools that are used to measure weather. Our class has learned that different tools are used for temperature, wind direction, and rain amounts. We have also learned how clouds form and the different types of wet weather. The children have also investigated the differences in the seasons.

While learning about weather, the children have also learned many new vocabulary words. Help your child to make these words a part of his or her own vocabulary by using them when you talk together about weather.

weather
temperature
thermometer
water vapor
clouds
sleet
season

These following pages include activities that you and your child can do together. By participating in your child's education, you will help to bring the learning home.

Look at the pictures and words below. **Draw** lines to match the weather tools on the left with the kind of weather they measure on the right.

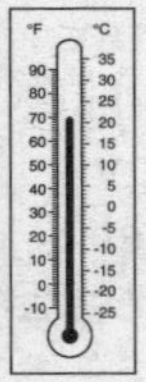

wind direction

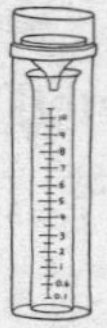

temperature

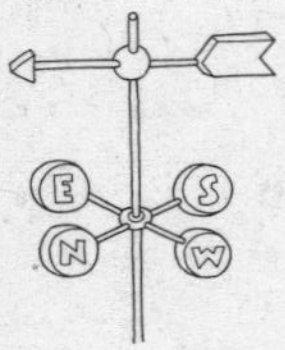

how much rain falls

Fun Fact

Hail is a type of wet weather. Hail is small pieces of ice. Hail falls from clouds as rain. The rain turns to hail when it moves through very cold air. Hail can be dangerous. It is important to stay inside when it hails.

© Pearson Education, Inc.

The Four Seasons

Color leaves on each tree to show how they look during each season.

spring

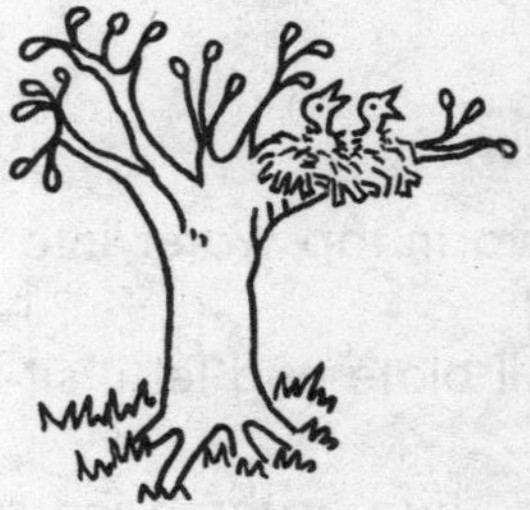

summer

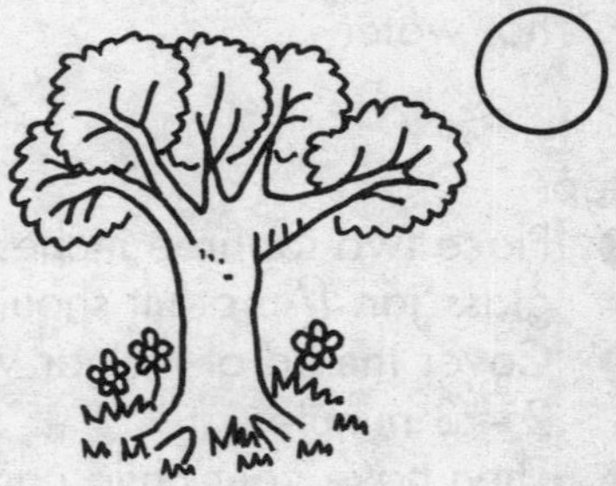

fall

winter

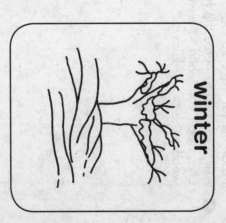

Name ______________________________

Use with Chapter 8.

Draw a picture or write a sentence to go with each word.

matter	solid
liquid	dissolve
gas	evaporate

© Pearson Education, Inc.

Directions: Read the words and draw pictures to illustrate them or write sentences about them. Cut out the boxes to use as word cards.
Home Activity: Discuss with your child how the three states of matter—solid, liquid, gas—are alike and different and name examples of each. To reinforce the definitions of *dissolve* and *evaporate,* use salt and water to demonstrate the meaning of each word.

Name ______________________________

Use with Chapter 8.

Alike and Different

Read the science story.
Look at the picture.
Fill in the chart on the next page.

A Ball and a Balloon

Look at the ball and the balloon. The ball is round and blue. It is filled with air. It feels smooth on the outside. The balloon is also filled with air. It feels smooth on the outside. But it is long and green.

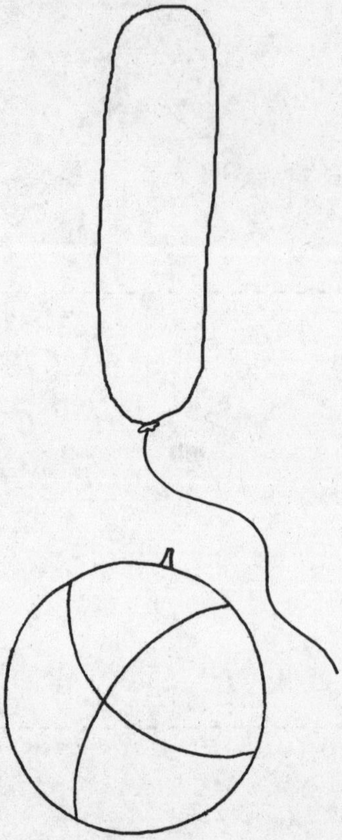

© Pearson Education, Inc.

Name ______________________________

Use with Chapter 8.

Apply It!

Communicate Tell how the ball and the balloon are alike and different. Write in the boxes.

Alike	Different

© Pearson Education, Inc.

Directions: Read the Science Story and look at the picture. Think about how the ball and the balloon are alike. Write those details under *Alike* in the chart. Think about how the ball and the balloon are different. Write those details under *Different* in the chart.

Home Activity: Your child learned about the concept of alike and different. Choose two kinds of fruits, vegetables, cans, or utensils from your kitchen. Ask your child to tell how the two items are alike and different.

Notes

Name ____________________________

Use with pages 215–217.

What is matter?

Before You Read Lesson 1

Read each sentence. Do you think it is true? Do you think it is not true? Circle the word or words after each sentence that tell what you think.

1. A cup is made of matter.	True	Not True
2. Matter takes up space.	True	Not True
3. Some parts of matter are too small to see without a hand lens.	True	Not True

After You Read Lesson 1

Read each sentence again. Circle the word or words after each sentence that tell what you think now. Did you change any answers? Put an **X** by each answer that you changed.

1. A cup is made of matter.	True	Not True
2. Matter takes up space.	True	Not True
3. Some parts of matter are too small to see without a hand lens.	True	Not True

© Pearson Education, Inc.

Home Activity: Together talk about your child's answers. Have your child explain why his or her answers may have changed after reading the lesson.

Name ______________________

Use with pages 215–217.

Complete the Sentence

Write the word that completes each sentence.

small	matter	mass	parts

1. If something takes up space, it is made of ______________.

2. Matter has many tiny ______________.

3. Matter has ______________.

4. Things can be sizes like big or ______________.

Draw Conclusions

5. Look at the picture and write down four things that are made of matter.

______________________ ______________________

______________________ ______________________

Name ______________________________

Use with pages 218–221.

What are solids, liquids, and gases?

Before You Read Lesson 2

Read each sentence. Do you think it is true? Do you think it is not true? Circle the word or words after each sentence that tell what you think.

1. A solid does not change shape when it is moved. True Not True
2. Liquids have their own shapes. True Not True
3. Solids and gases take up space. True Not True

After You Read Lesson 2

Read each sentence again. Circle the word or words after each sentence that tell what you think now. Did you change any answers? Put an **X** by each answer that you changed.

1. A solid does not change shape when it is moved. True Not True
2. Liquids have their own shapes. True Not True
3. Solids and gases take up space. True Not True

© Pearson Education, Inc.

Home Activity: Together talk about your child's answers. Have your child explain why his or her answers may have changed after reading the lesson.

Name ______________________________

Use with pages 218–221.

Complete the Sentence

Write the word that completes each sentence.

liquid	space	gas	solid

1. A ______________ has a shape that does not change.

2. A ______________ is wet and changes shape.

3. You cannot see ______________, but it can change its shape.

4. All kinds of matter take up ______________.

Alike and Different

5. Write how the things below are alike and different.

is a solid   is long   is round   is hard

Ball	Baseball Bat
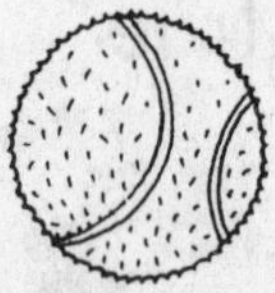	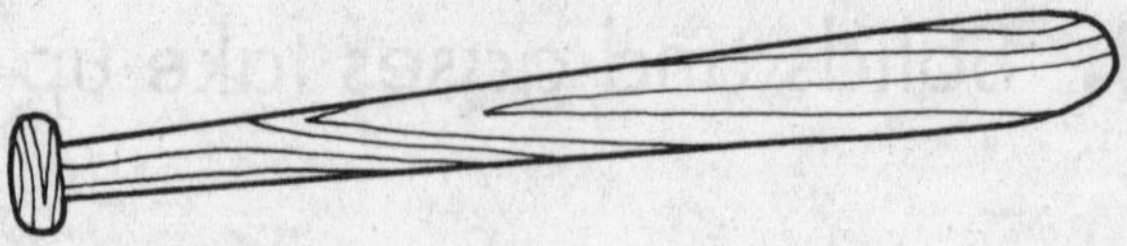

Name ______________________________

Use with pages 222–225.

How does matter change?

Before You Read Lesson 3

Read each sentence. Do you think it is true? Do you think it is not true? Circle the word or words after each sentence that tell what you think.

1.	Heat cannot change a solid.	True	Not True
2.	Solids and liquids can be mixed.	True	Not True
3.	Salt will dissolve in water.	True	Not True

After You Read Lesson 3

Read each sentence again. Circle the word or words after each sentence that tell what you think now. Did you change any answers? Put an **X** by each answer that you changed.

1.	Heat cannot change a solid.	True	Not True
2.	Solids and liquids can be mixed.	True	Not True
3.	Salt will dissolve in water.	True	Not True

© Pearson Education, Inc.

Home Activity: Together talk about your child's answers. Have your child explain why his or her answers may have changed after reading the lesson.

Name ______________________

Use with pages 222–225.

Complete the Sentence

Write the word that completes each sentence.

melt	mix	freeze	dissolve

1. When a liquid gets very cold, it can ____________.
2. When a solid gets hot, it will ____________.
3. You can ____________ matter together to make something new.
4. Some solids, like salt, can ____________ in a liquid.

Picture Clues

5. Use the picture clues to tell what is happening to the ice cream cone.

Name ______________________________

Use with pages 226–229.

How can water change?

Before You Read Lesson 4

Read each sentence. Do you think it is true? Do you think it is not true? Circle the word or words after each sentence that tell what you think.

1.	Water is a liquid.	True	Not True
2.	Water can change into a gas.	True	Not True
3.	*Evaporate* means to change from a solid to a liquid.	True	Not True

After You Read Lesson 4

Read each sentence again. Circle the word or words after each sentence that tell what you think now. Did you change any answers? Put an **X** by each answer that you changed.

1.	Water is a liquid.	True	Not True
2.	Water can change into a gas.	True	Not True
3.	*Evaporate* means to change from a solid to a liquid.	True	Not True

© Pearson Education, Inc.

Home Activity: Together talk about your child's answers. Have your child explain why his or her answers may have changed after reading the lesson.

Name ______________________________

Use with pages 226–229.

Complete the Sentence

Write the word that completes each sentence.

freeze	melt	evaporate	boil

1. When water gets very hot, it will __________.

2. To make ice, water must __________.

3. Ice can __________ and become a liquid.

4. The Sun can make water __________ and change into a gas.

Put Things in Order

5. Write on the lines what happens to water first, next, and last.

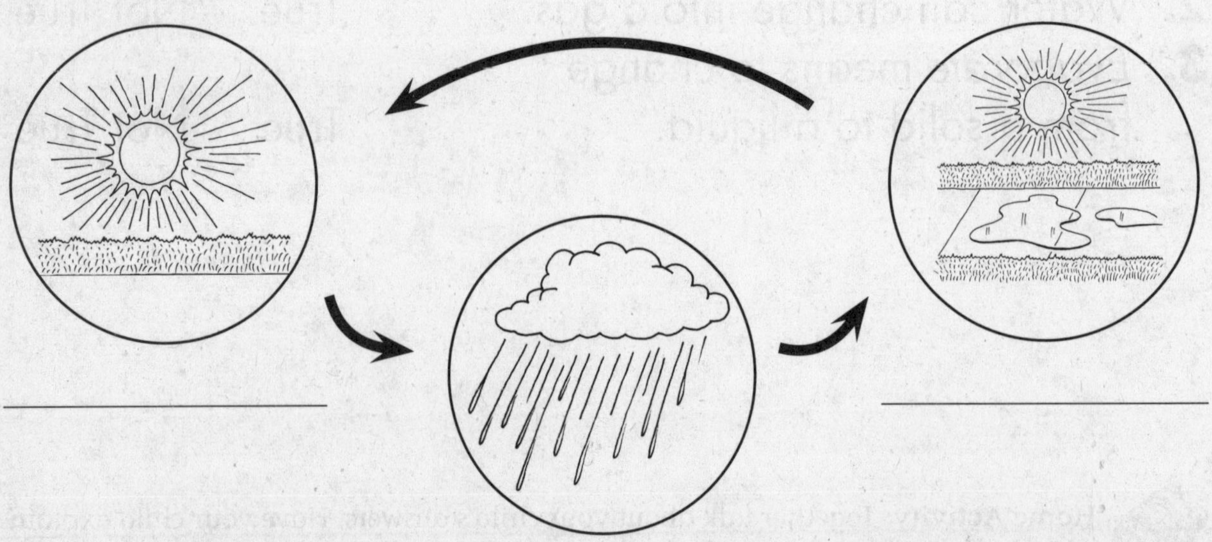

__________ __________ __________

Name ______________________________

Use with pages 230–231.

What are other ways matter changes?

Before You Read Lesson 5

Read each sentence. Do you think it is true? Do you think it is not true? Circle the word or words after each sentence that tell what you think.

1. One kind of matter can change into another kind.	True	Not True
2. Iron can change into rust.	True	Not True
3. Paper does not change when it is burned.	True	Not True

After You Read Lesson 5

Read each sentence again. Circle the word or words after each sentence that tell what you think now. Did you change any answers? Put an **X** by each answer that you changed.

1. One kind of matter can change into another kind.	True	Not True
2. Iron can change into rust.	True	Not True
3. Paper does not change when it is burned.	True	Not True

© Pearson Education, Inc.

Home Activity: Together talk about your child's answers. Have your child explain why his or her answers may have changed after reading the lesson.

Name ______________________

Use with pages 230–231.

Complete the Sentence

Write the word that completes each sentence.

burn	change	ash	color

1. Some kinds of matter can ____________ into new matter.

2. Fire can make wood ____________.

3. After the fire, the wood will become ____________.

4. Some matter will turn a different ____________.

Picture Clues

5. Use picture clues to tell what change is happening in the picture below.

Name ______________________________

Use with Chapter 8.

Comparing Height and Weight

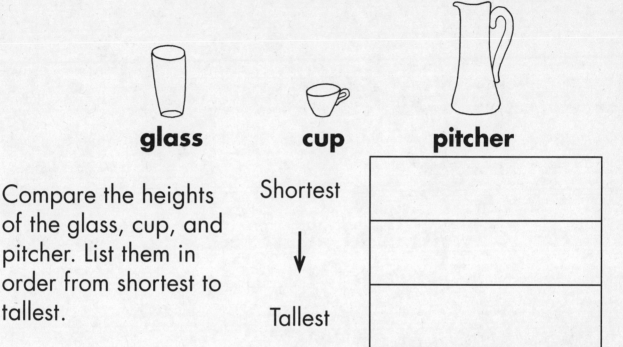

glass

cup

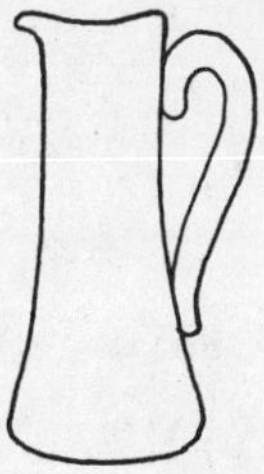
pitcher

Compare the heights of the glass, cup, and pitcher. List them in order from shortest to tallest.

Shortest
↓
Tallest

bowl

cup

pot

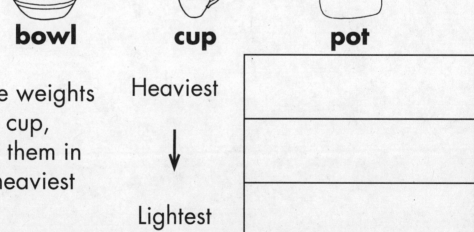

Compare the weights of the bowl, cup, and pot. List them in order from heaviest to lightest.

Heaviest
↓
Lightest

Directions: Look at the first set of pictures. Think about putting the objects in order from shortest to tallest. Write the names of the objects in that order in the boxes. Do the same with the second set of pictures, arranging them in order from heaviest to lightest.

Home Activity: Your child learned about comparing the heights and weights of objects. Choose sets of three household objects of varying heights and weights. Have your child put the objects in order from shortest to tallest or heaviest to lightest.

© Pearson Education, Inc.

Notes

Family Science Activity

Where did it go?

Materials
- 3 clear glasses
- salt
- sugar
- pepper
- tablespoon
- stirring spoon
- water

Steps
1. Fill each glass about two-thirds full of water.
2. In the first glass add one tablespoon of salt and stir for one minute.
3. Repeat Step 2 using sugar and pepper with the other two glasses.
4. Encourage your child to observe what happened to each type of solid that was added to the water. Have your child describe the results using their own words.
5. Have your child identify other solids from the kitchen that will dissolve or will not dissolve in water.

© Pearson Education, Inc.

Use with Chapter 8

Dear Family,

Your child is learning what matter is and how it can be described and changed. In the science chapter Observing Matter, our class has learned the differences between a solid, a liquid, and a gas. We have also learned how matter can change. The children have also learned that water turns to ice when it gets very cold and water vapor when it gets very hot.

In addition to learning how to describe matter and how matter changes, the children have also learned many new vocabulary words. Help your child to make these words a part of his or her own vocabulary by using them when you talk together about different types of matter.

matter
solid
liquid
gas
dissolve
evaporate

These following pages include activities that you and your child can do together. By participating in your child's education, you will help to bring the learning home.

Fill in each sentence with the correct word from the box.

dissolve
evaporate
freeze

1 When the Sun shines, a puddle of water will ____________.

2 Water will ____________ when it gets very cold.

3 Salt will ____________ in a glass of water.

Fun Fact

Salt that is dissolved in water can be taken out again. If you leave a glass of salt water on the counter, the water evaporates. When the water evaporates, the salt is left in the glass. When all the water evaporates, all you will have is salt in the glass.

© Pearson Education, Inc.

Literacy and Art

Look for solids in the picture.
Color the solids with crayons.

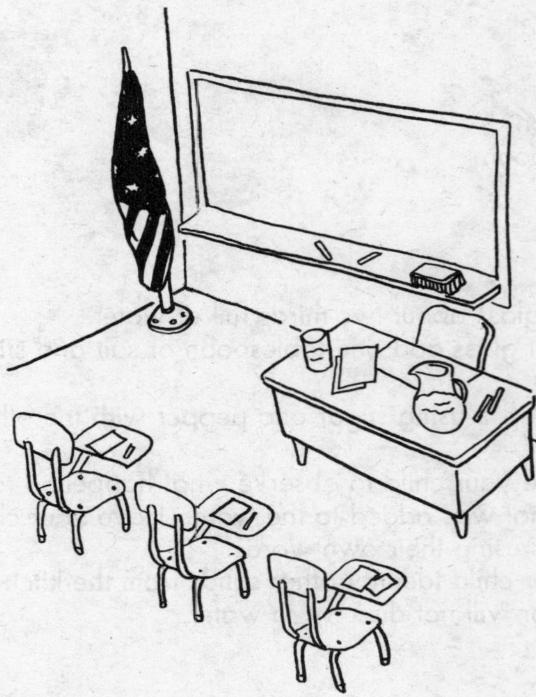

Fun Idea

Where is the liquid in the picture? You may color the liquid with a blue crayon.

Name ____________________

Use with Chapter 9.

Draw a picture or write a sentence to go with each word.

magnet	force
attract	gravity
repel	speed
pole	vibrate

© Pearson Education, Inc.

Directions: Read the words and draw pictures to illustrate them or write sentences about them. Cut out the boxes to use as word cards.
Home Activity: Review the vocabulary words with your child. Then make up a sentence for each word, leaving the word out and letting your child say the word.

Name ______________________________

Cause and Effect

Read the science story.
Look at the picture.
Make a prediction.

Moving a Ball

The boy causes the ball to move by throwing it.

© Pearson Education, Inc.

Name ____________________________

Use with Chapter 9.

Apply It!

Predict. What will the girl do? Tell what effect that will have on the ball.

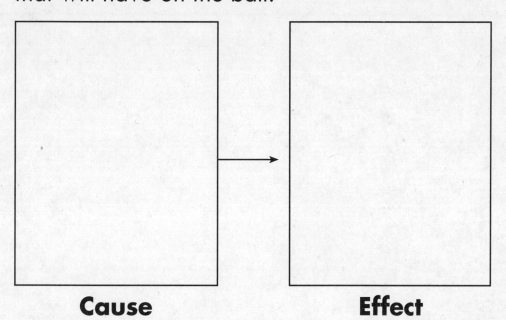

Cause → **Effect**

© Pearson Education, Inc.

Directions: Read the Science Story and look at the picture. Think about what is happening. Then predict what the girl will do and what will happen to the ball.
Home Activity: Your child learned about the concept of cause and effect. Flip a light switch. Turn a doorknob. Drop a book. Each time ask your child what effect your action has. *(The light comes on. The door opens. The book is on the floor.)*

Notes

Name ____________________

Use with pages 247–249.

What makes things move?

Before You Read Lesson 1

Read each sentence. Do you think it is true? Do you think it is not true? Circle the word or words after each sentence that tell what you think.

1.	Force makes things move.	True	Not True
2.	Gravity makes things go up in the air.	True	Not True
3.	We can use a little or a lot of force.	True	Not True

After You Read Lesson 1

Read each sentence again. Circle the word or words after each sentence that tell what you think now. Did you change any answers? Put an **X** by each answer that you changed.

1.	Force makes things move.	True	Not True
2.	Gravity makes things go up in the air.	True	Not True
3.	We can use a little or a lot of force.	True	Not True

© Pearson Education, Inc.

Home Activity: Together talk about your child's answers. Have your child explain why his or her answers may have changed after reading the lesson.

Name ______________________

Use with pages 247–249.

Complete the Sentence

Write the word that completes each sentence.

gravity	heavy	force	pull

1. To make something move you use __________.

2. You have to try hard to move something __________.

3. You can __________ a sled.

4. The force that keeps you and other things on the ground is called __________.

Picture Clues

5. Use picture clues and color the picture where force is being used.

Name ____________________

Think, Read, Learn

Use with pages 250–251.

What is speed?

Before You Read Lesson 2

Read each sentence. Do you think it is true? Do you think it is not true? Circle the word or words after each sentence that tell what you think.

1. Speed is how far away something moves.	True	Not True
2. Force can change the way things move.	True	Not True
3. Less force causes less speed.	True	Not True

After You Read Lesson 2

Read each sentence again. Circle the word or words after each sentence that tell what you think now. Did you change any answers? Put an **X** by each answer that you changed.

1. Speed is how far away something moves.	True	Not True
2. Force can change the way things move.	True	Not True
3. Less force causes less speed.	True	Not True

© Pearson Education, Inc.

Home Activity: Together talk about your child's answers. Have your child explain why his or her answers may have changed after reading the lesson.

Name ______________________

Use with pages 250–251.

Complete the Sentence

Write the word that completes each sentence.
Use each word twice.

force	speed

1. How fast or slow something moves is __________.

2. You can use __________ to change the way things move.

3. More __________ will make something go faster.

4. A moving car has a faster __________ than a person walking.

Draw Conclusions

5. Look at the picture and write which person would have the faster speed.

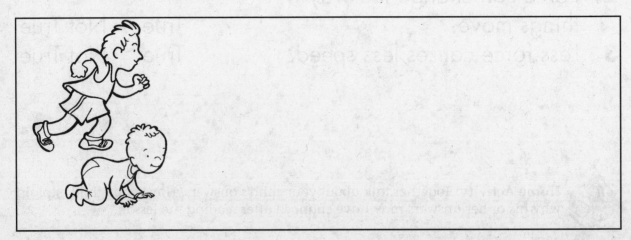

Name ______________________________

Use with pages 252–255.

How do things move?

Before You Read Lesson 3

Read each sentence. Do you think it is true? Do you think it is not true? Circle the word or words after each sentence that tell what you think.

1.	A ball can only move in a straight line.	True	Not True
2.	A car can move around curves.	True	Not True
3.	A block in the middle is between two other blocks.	True	Not True

After You Read Lesson 3

Read each sentence again. Circle the word or words after each sentence that tell what you think now. Did you change any answers? Put an **X** by each answer that you changed.

1.	A ball can only move in a straight line.	True	Not True
2.	A car can move around curves.	True	Not True
3.	A block in the middle is between two other blocks.	True	Not True

© Pearson Education, Inc.

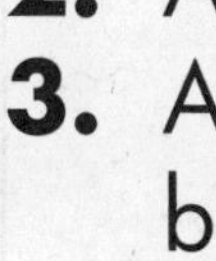

Home Activity: Together talk about your child's answers. Have your child explain why his or her answers may have changed after reading the lesson.

Name ______________________________

Lesson 3 Review

Use with pages 252–255.

Complete the Sentence

Write the word that completes each sentence.

up	left	curve	places

1. A ball can bounce ____________ and down.
2. A car can drive straight or around a ____________.
3. Things can move ____________ and right.
4. The words *top* and *bottom* tell about ____________.

Cause and Effect

5. Look at the picture and write what would cause the boy to move back and forth.

Name ______________________________

Use with pages 256–259.

What do magnets do?

Before You Read Lesson 4

Read each sentence. Do you think it is true? Do you think it is not true? Circle the word or words after each sentence that tell what you think.

1. Magnets attract things made of iron. True Not True
2. *Repel* means to pull toward. True Not True
3. The north poles of two magnets will repel each other. True Not True

After You Read Lesson 4

Read each sentence again. Circle the word or words after each sentence that tell what you think now. Did you change any answers? Put an **X** by each answer that you changed.

1. Magnets attract things made of iron. True Not True
2. *Repel* means to pull toward. True Not True
3. The north poles of two magnets will repel each other. True Not True

© Pearson Education, Inc.

Home Activity: Together talk about your child's answers. Have your child explain why his or her answers may have changed after reading the lesson.

Name ______________________________

Use with pages 256–259.

Complete the Sentence

Write the word that completes each sentence.

attract	repel	magnet	pole

1. A ______________ can attract metal.

2. Two things can ______________, or pull toward, each other.

3. A north and a south ______________ pull toward each other.

4. Two things can ______________, or push away from, each other.

Predict

5. Predict what object the magnet will attract. Color the object.

Magnet	Objects
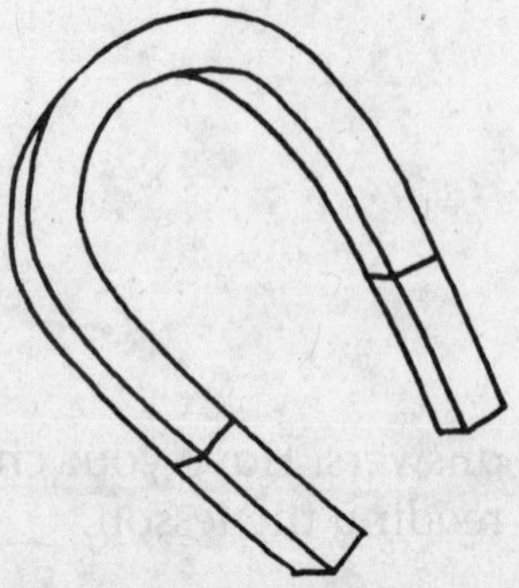	

Name ______________________________

Use with pages 260–261.

How are sounds made?

Before You Read Lesson 5

Read each sentence. Do you think it is true? Do you think it is not true? Circle the word or words after each sentence that tell what you think.

1. A sound is made when something vibrates.	True	Not True
2. A banjo string vibrates when you pluck it.	True	Not True
3. Sounds are always loud.	True	Not True

After You Read Lesson 5

Read each sentence again. Circle the word or words after each sentence that tell what you think now. Did you change any answers? Put an X by each answer that you changed.

1. A sound is made when something vibrates.	True	Not True
2. A banjo string vibrates when you pluck it.	True	Not True
3. Sounds are always loud.	True	Not True

© Pearson Education, Inc.

Home Activity: Together talk about your child's answers. Have your child explain why his or her answers may have changed after reading the lesson.

Name ______________________________

Use with pages 260–261.

Complete the Sentence

Write the word that completes each sentence.

fast	force	vibrate	soft

1. A thing needs to ______________ to make sounds.

2. You must use ______________ to make a sound.

3. Sounds can be loud or ______________.

4. A thing must move back and forth ______________ to make a sound.

Cause and Effect

5. Write the effect of hitting the drum.

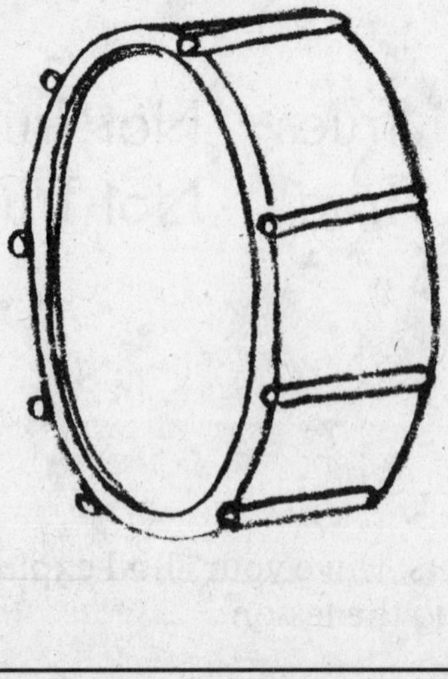

Name ______________________________

Use with pages 262–265.

What sounds are around us?

Before You Read Lesson 6

Read each sentence. Do you think it is true? Do you think it is not true? Circle the word or words after each sentence that tell what you think.

1. Honks and beeps tell you to be careful.	True	Not True
2. Fire trucks and police cars make loud sounds.	True	Not True
3. You can hear sounds in nature.	True	Not True

After You Read Lesson 6

Read each sentence again. Circle the word or words after each sentence that tell what you think now. Did you change any answers? Put an **X** by each answer that you changed.

1. Honks and beeps tell you to be careful.	True	Not True
2. Fire trucks and police cars make loud sounds.	True	Not True
3. You can hear sounds in nature.	True	Not True

© Pearson Education, Inc.

Home Activity: Together talk about your child's answers. Have your child explain why his or her answers may have changed after reading the lesson.

Name ______________________

Use with pages 262–265.

Complete the Sentence

Write the word that completes each sentence.

honk	crashing	sirens	chirping

1. Car horns ____________.

2. Birds make ____________ sounds.

3. Fire trucks have loud ____________.

4. The ocean makes a ____________ sound on the rocks.

Draw Conclusions

5. Write if the thing in each picture makes a loud or a soft sound.

Butterfly	Lion	Bus

____________ sound	____________ sound	____________ sound

Name ______________________

Speed

girl **baby** **boy**

Compare the speeds of the girl, baby, and boy. List them in order from slowest to fastest.

Slowest

↓

Fastest

raccoon **beetle** **deer**

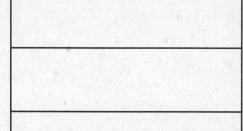

Compare the speeds of the raccoon, beetle, and deer. List them in order from fastest to slowest.

Fastest

↓

Slowest

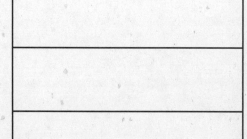

Directions: Look at the first set of pictures. Think about putting the people in order from slowest to fastest. Write the words in that order in the boxes. Do the same with the animals, arranging them in order from fastest to slowest.
Home Activity: Your child learned that different things move at different speeds. Find pairs of magazine pictures that show people and machines moving and ask your child which moves faster or which moves slower.

© Pearson Education, Inc.

Notes

Family Science Activity

Does It Stick?

Materials
- 2 refrigerator magnets
- several metal household items
- several nonmetal household items

Steps
1. Have both you and your child take one of the refrigerator magnets.
2. Have the magnets facing each other and ask your child to tell if the magnets attract or repel each other. Encourage your child to describe the poles of each magnet.
3. Together, see if the magnet attracts, repels, or has no effect on various household items.
4. Ask your child to describe what happens to the magnet for each household item. Have your child group the items based on whether the magnet attracts, repels, or has no effect on them.

© Pearson Education, Inc.

Take Home Booklet

Use with Chapter 9

Dear Family,

In the science chapter Movement and Sound, our class is learning how forces cause movement. The children have also studied how to describe the speed of an object and how an object moves. We have also learned about the special forces magnets have. Further, the children explored how movements called vibrations make sound.

In addition to learning about movement and sound, the children have also learned many new vocabulary words. Help your child to make these words a part of his or her own vocabulary by using them when you talk together about movement and sound.

force
gravity
speed
magnet
attract
pole
repel
vibrate

These following pages include activities that you and your child can do together. By participating in your child's education, you will help to bring the learning home.

An Apple Tree

Read the sentences.
Draw a picture in the box using the sentences.

An apple tree is in a field.
The Sun is above the tree.
The grass is below the tree.
An apple is falling from the tree.

© Pearson Education, Inc.

Roller Coaster Movement

Trace the path of the roller coaster around the track.
Use the words in the word box to tell how the roller coaster moves.

up
down
right
left
straight line
curve

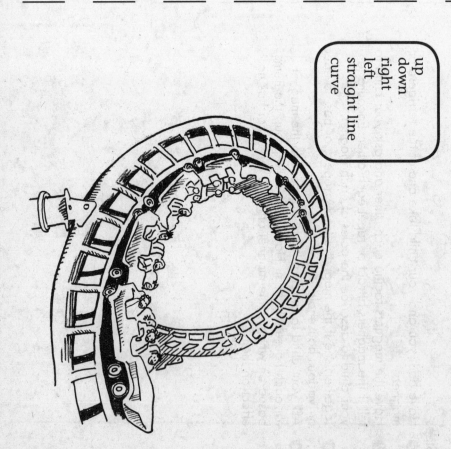

Name ______________________

Vocabulary Preview

Use with Chapter 10.

Draw a picture or write a sentence to go with each word.

energy	electricity
heat	fuel
shadow	battery

© Pearson Education, Inc.

Directions: Read the words and draw pictures to illustrate them or write sentences about them. Cut out the boxes to use as word cards.
Home Activity: Make up a sentence using a vocabulary word. Say the sentence to your child, leaving out the vocabulary word and having your child complete the sentence. Continue with the other vocabulary words.

Name ______________________

Use with Chapter 10.

Cause and Effect

Read the science story.
Look at the picture.
Fill in the chart to answer the question.

Going Outside

Anna puts on her coat. She puts on her hat and gloves. She wraps her scarf around her face and neck. She is getting ready to go outside.

© Pearson Education, Inc.

Name ________________________________

Use with Chapter 10.

Apply It!

Infer What is the weather like outside?

I know.	→	**My conclusion.**

Directions: Read the story and look at the picture. Use what the story and picture tell you, as well as what you already know about weather and clothing, to fill in the *I know* box. Then use that information to fill in the *My conclusion* box.

Home Activity: Your child learned about drawing conclusions. Show items such as an umbrella, sunglasses, and a sweater one at a time. Ask your child what conclusion he or she can draw about the weather if someone has that item.

© Pearson Education, Inc.

Notes

Name ______________________________

Use with pages 279–281.

What gives off heat?

Before You Read Lesson 1

Read each sentence. Do you think it is true? Do you think it is not true? Circle the word or words after each sentence that tell what you think.

1. Light from the Sun warms Earth's air, water, and land.	True	Not True
2. Heat can come from fire.	True	Not True
3. Rubbing your hands together does not make heat.	True	Not True

After You Read Lesson 1

Read each sentence again. Circle the word or words after each sentence that tell what you think now. Did you change any answers? Put an **X** by each answer that you changed.

1. Light from the Sun warms Earth's air, water, and land.	True	Not True
2. Heat can come from fire.	True	Not True
3. Rubbing your hands together does not make heat.	True	Not True

© Pearson Education, Inc.

Home Activity: Together talk about your child's answers. Have your child explain why his or her answers may have changed after reading the lesson.

Name ______________________

Use with pages 279–281.

Complete the Sentence

Write the word that completes each sentence.

Sun	heat	Fire	water

1. Anything that gives off ______________ makes other things warm.

2. The light from the ______________ can warm things.

3. That light can heat ______________.

4. ______________ burns and makes things warm.

Picture Clues

5. Use picture clues and color the pictures of things giving off heat.

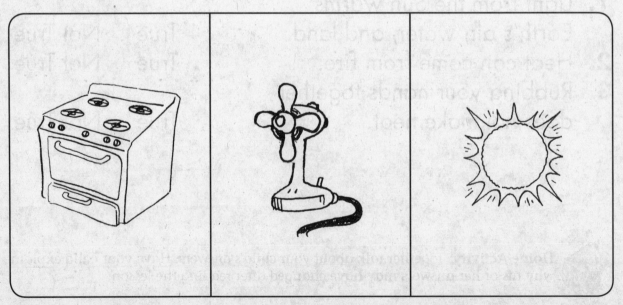

Name ______________________________

Use with pages 282–283.

What can energy do?

Before You Read Lesson 2

Read each sentence. Do you think it is true? Do you think it is not true? Circle the word or words after each sentence that tell what you think.

1. Energy from the Sun can change the temperature. True Not True
2. Dark colors take in less energy from the Sun. True Not True
3. A black shirt is warmer than a white shirt. True Not True

After You Read Lesson 2

Read each sentence again. Circle the word or words after each sentence that tell what you think now. Did you change any answers? Put an **X** by each answer that you changed.

1. Energy from the Sun can change the temperature. True Not True
2. Dark colors take in less energy from the Sun. True Not True
3. A black shirt is warmer than a white shirt. True Not True

© Pearson Education, Inc.

Home Activity: Together talk about your child's answers. Have your child explain why his or her answers may have changed after reading the lesson.

Name ______________________

Use with pages 282–283.

Complete the Sentence

Write the word that completes each sentence.

light	temperature	energy	dark

1. Something that can change things is ____________.

2. The Sun can change the ______________ outside.

3. If you wear ______________ colors, you will stay cool.

4. If you wear ______________ colors, you will get hot.

Draw Conclusions

5. Look at the picture and write which person will stay cooler.

I know	I conclude

Name ______________________________

Use with pages 284–289.

What makes light and shadows?

Before You Read Lesson 3

Read each sentence. Do you think it is true? Do you think it is not true? Circle the word or words after each sentence that tell what you think.

1. Light can pass through everything. True Not True
2. You make a shadow when you block the light. True Not True
3. Shadows are short at noon. True Not True

After You Read Lesson 3

Read each sentence again. Circle the word or words after each sentence that tell what you think now. Did you change any answers? Put an **X** by each answer that you changed.

1. Light can pass through everything. True Not True
2. You make a shadow when you block the light. True Not True
3. Shadows are short at noon. True Not True

© Pearson Education, Inc.

Home Activity: Together talk about your child's answers. Have your child explain why his or her answers may have changed after reading the lesson.

Name ______________________

Use with pages 284–289.

Complete the Sentence

Write the word that completes each sentence.

Sun	shadow	window	high

1. Fire and the ______________ both can make light.
2. Light can pass through a ______________.
3. When light cannot pass through something, it makes a ______________.
4. The Sun is ______________ in the sky at noon.

Cause and Effect

5. Look at the picture and write what is causing the shadow.

Cause

Name ______________________________

Use with pages 290–293.

What uses energy around us?

Before You Read Lesson 4

Read each sentence. Do you think it is true? Do you think it is not true? Circle the word or words after each sentence that tell what you think.

1. Cars get energy from gasoline. True Not True
2. Many things get energy from electricity. True Not True
3. Electricity cannot be stored. True Not True

After You Read Lesson 4

Read each sentence again. Circle the word or words after each sentence that tell what you think now. Did you change any answers? Put an **X** by each answer that you changed.

1. Cars get energy from gasoline. True Not True
2. Many things get energy from electricity. True Not True
3. Electricity cannot be stored. True Not True

© Pearson Education, Inc.

Home Activity: Together talk about your child's answers. Have your child explain why his or her answers may have changed after reading the lesson.

Name ______________________

Use with pages 290–293.

Complete the Sentence

Write the word that completes each sentence.

electricity	heat	fuel	battery

1. One form of energy is ____________.

2. A ____________ stores electricity.

3. Cars burn ____________ to get energy.

4. Burning something makes ____________.

Important Details

5. Write two important details you learned about how a lamp works.

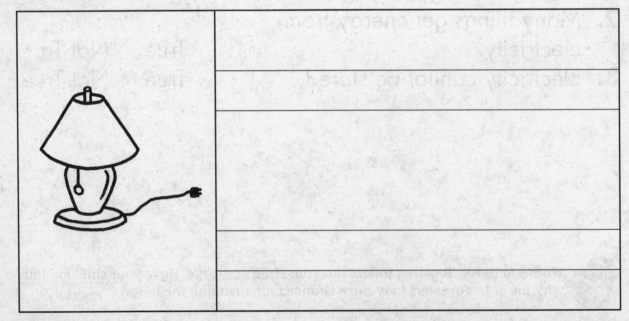

Name ________________________________

Use with pages 294–297.

How do you get energy?

Before You Read Lesson 5

Read each sentence. Do you think it is true? Do you think it is not true? Circle the word or words after each sentence that tell what you think.

1.	You eat food to get energy.	True	Not True
2.	You need to eat many kinds of food.	True	Not True
3.	You do not use energy when you sleep.	True	Not True

After You Read Lesson 5

Read each sentence again. Circle the word or words after each sentence that tell what you think now. Did you change any answers? Put an **X** by each answer that you changed.

1.	You eat food to get energy.	True	Not True
2.	You need to eat many kinds of food.	True	Not True
3.	You do not use energy when you sleep.	True	Not True

© Pearson Education, Inc.

Home Activity: Together talk about your child's answers. Have your child explain why his or her answers may have changed after reading the lesson.

Name ______________________

Use with pages 294–297.

Complete the Sentence

Write the word that completes each sentence.

strong	move	food	grow

1. Energy helps people ____________ and play.

2. The right ____________ can give you energy.

3. Milk can make your bones ____________.

4. With energy, your body can ____________.

Alike and Different

5. Write about the ways that people and cars get and use energy that are alike and different.

eat food   use fuel   need energy to move

People	**Cars**

Name ______________________________

Use with Chapter 10.

Reading a Picture Graph

Max asked people to name their favorite vegetable.
The picture graph shows what people said.

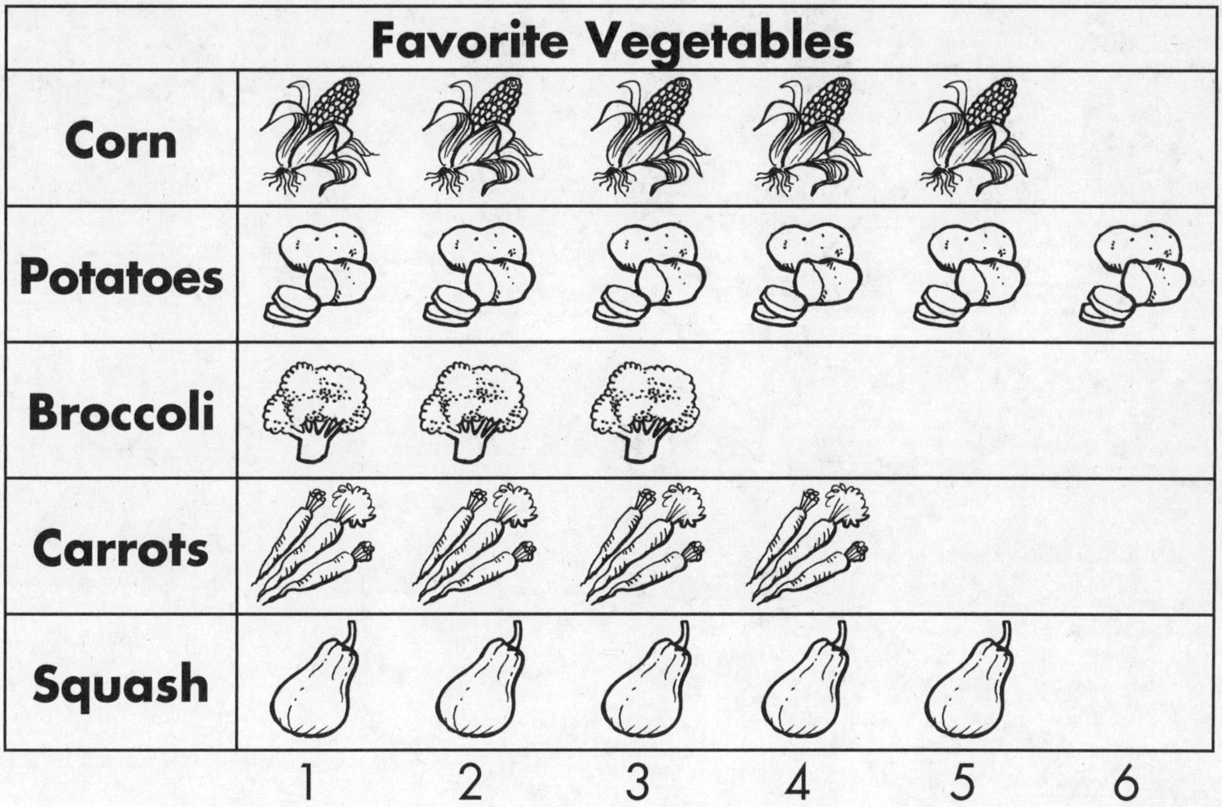

Use the picture graph to answer the questions.

1. Which vegetables were chosen by the same number of people? ____________________

2. How many more people chose potatoes than carrots? ____________________

Directions: On the picture graph, each picture of a vegetable stands for one person who chose that vegetable as his or her favorite. Count the pictures in each row. Then answer the questions using those numbers.
Home Activity: Your child learned how to read a picture graph. Ask your child to explain how he or she answered the questions about the graph. Then ask other questions, such as *How many people chose squash? Which vegetable was chosen by the fewest people?*

© Pearson Education, Inc.

Notes

Family Science Activity

Changing Shadows

Materials

- Three colors of chalk

Steps

1. First thing in the morning, go outside with your child. On the ground, trace your child's shadow using the chalk. Also, draw a line around your child's feet to mark the area where he or she was standing.
2. At noon, repeat the activity with your child. Be sure your child stands in the same spot from the morning activity. Use a different colored chalk to make the outline.
3. Repeat the activity one more time prior to dinner. Again, be sure your child stands in the same location. Use a third color of chalk to make the outline.
4. Discuss with your child how the shadow was made. Explain that his or her body blocked the light of the Sun, which created the shadow.
5. Talk about how the shadow outline changed as the Sun changed positions in the sky.

© Pearson Education, Inc.

Dear Family,

In the science chapter Learning About Energy, our class is learning that there are different kinds of energy. We have also learned about light and shadows. The children have also studied the different ways people use energy and how things around us also use energy.

In addition to learning about energy, the children have also learned many new vocabulary words. Help your child to make these words a part of his or her own vocabulary by using them when you talk together about energy.

heat
energy
shadow
fuel
electricity
battery

These following pages include activities that you and your child can do together. By participating in your child's education, you will help to bring the learning home.

How Do Things Get Energy?

Everything needs energy to work.
Draw a line from each picture on the left to show how it gets energy.

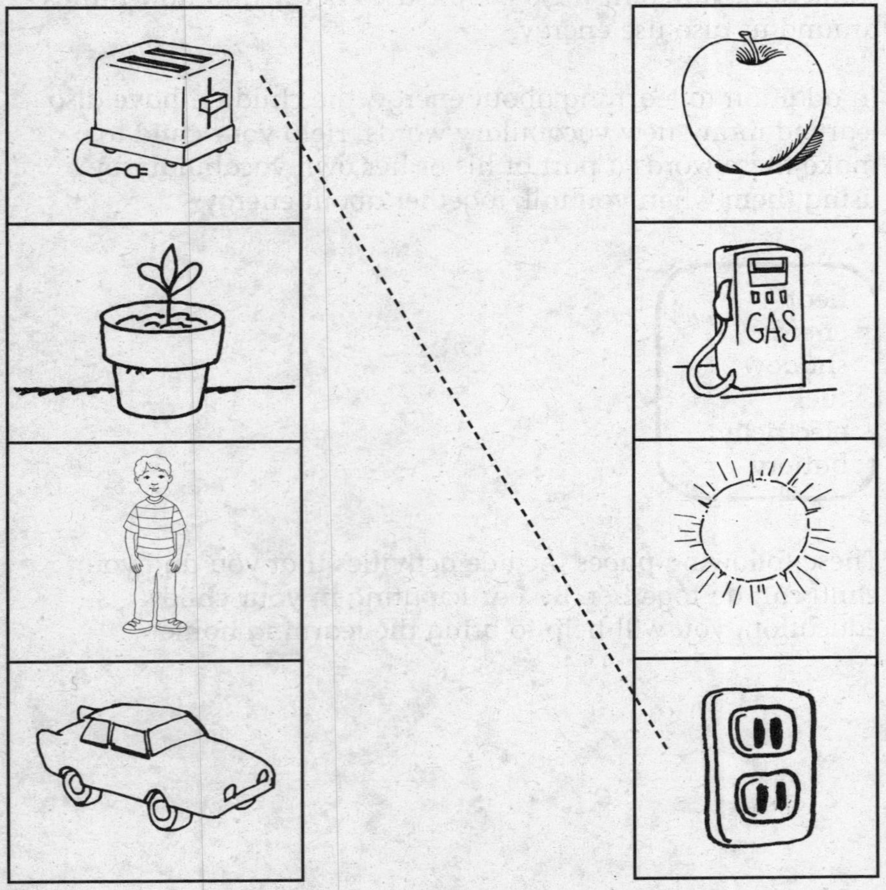

© Pearson Education, Inc.

What Gives Off Heat?

Color only the pictures that show things that give off heat.

Sun

Telephone

Fire

Lamp

Name ______________________________

Vocabulary Preview

Use with Chapter 11.

Draw a picture or write a sentence to go with each word.

Moon	rotation
Sun	planet
star	telescope

© Pearson Education, Inc.

Directions: Read the words and draw pictures to illustrate them or write sentences about them. Cut out the boxes to use as word cards.
Home Activity: Give a clue for each vocabulary word, such as *You see this during the day* or *You can look at stars with this,* and have your child give the correct word.

Use with Chapter 11.

Important Details

Read the science story.
Look at the picture.
Look for important details.

Stars

Look at the picture of the stars. Stars are balls of hot gases. They give off light. They look small because they are very far away.

Apply It!

Communicate Use the graphic organizer on the next page. List three important details you saw and read about stars.

© Pearson Education, Inc.

Name ______________________________

Use with Chapter 11.

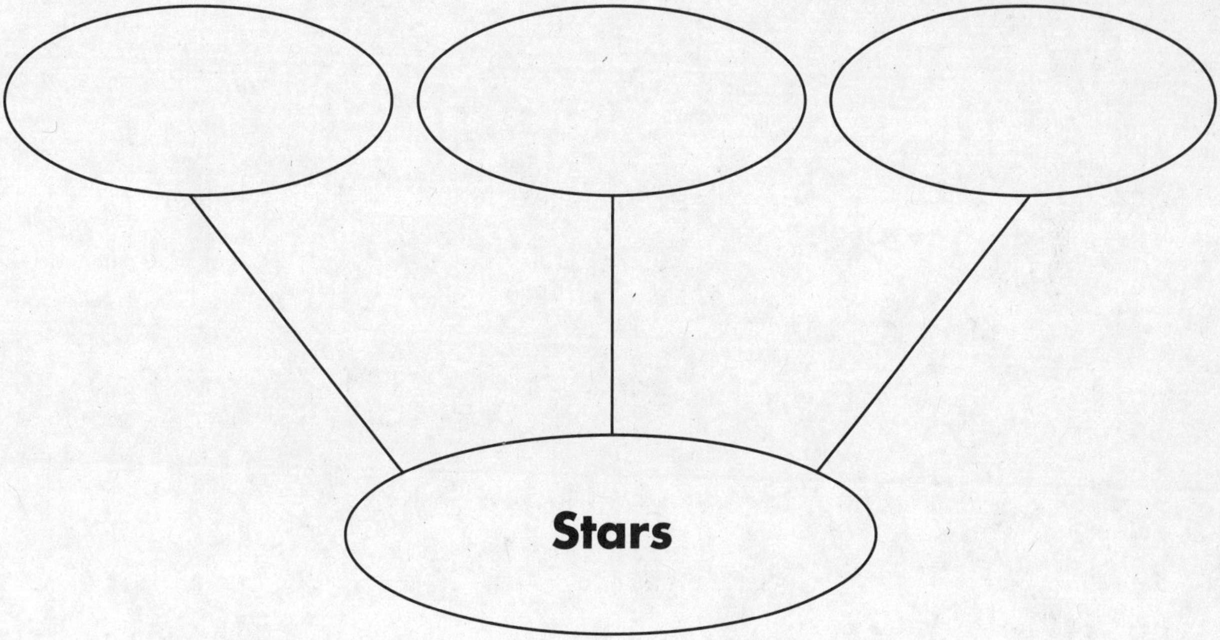

Directions: As you read the story and look at the picture, think about the important details. Ask yourself which details in the story and the picture tell you something. Then write those details in the chart.

Home Activity: Your child learned about recognizing important details in pictures and words. Together look at a picture in your child's textbook and decide what you think are important details in the picture.

© Pearson Education, Inc.

Notes

Name ______________________________

Use with pages 319–321.

What is in the day sky?

Before You Read Lesson 1

Read each sentence. Do you think it is true? Do you think it is not true? Circle the word or words after each sentence that tell what you think.

1. Living things need light from the Sun.	True	Not True
2. You never see the Moon in the day sky.	True	Not True
3. You see the Sun over your head at noon.	True	Not True

After You Read Lesson 1

Read each sentence again. Circle the word or words after each sentence that tell what you think now. Did you change any answers? Put an **X** by each answer that you changed.

1. Living things need light from the Sun.	True	Not True
2. You never see the Moon in the day sky.	True	Not True
3. You see the Sun over your head at noon.	True	Not True

© Pearson Education, Inc.

Home Activity: Together talk about your child's answers. Have your child explain why his or her answers may have changed after reading the lesson.

Name ______________________

Use with pages 319–321.

Complete the Sentence

Write the word that completes each sentence.

star	Sun	grow	Moon

1. The ____________ makes light in the daytime sky.

2. A hot ball of gas is called a ____________.

3. You can see the ____________ at night and sometimes in the day.

4. Living things ____________ because of light from the Sun.

Important Details

5. Write two important details you learned about the daytime sky.

Name ______________________________

Use with pages 322–323.

What causes day and night?

Before You Read Lesson 2

Read each sentence. Do you think it is true? Do you think it is not true? Circle the word or words after each sentence that tell what you think.

1.	Earth's turning causes day and night.	True	Not True
2.	It is night when your part of Earth faces away from the Sun.	True	Not True
3.	One part of Earth always faces the Sun.	True	Not True

After You Read Lesson 2

Read each sentence again. Circle the word or words after each sentence that tell what you think now. Did you change any answers? Put an **X** by each answer that you changed.

1.	Earth's turning causes day and night.	True	Not True
2.	It is night when your part of Earth faces away from the Sun.	True	Not True
3.	One part of Earth always faces the Sun.	True	Not True

© Pearson Education, Inc.

Home Activity: Together talk about your child's answers. Have your child explain why his or her answers may have changed after reading the lesson.

Name ______________________

Use with pages 322–323.

Complete the Sentence

Write the word that completes each sentence.

day	moving	rotation	night

1. Earth never stops ______________.

2. It is called ______________ when Earth turns around and around.

3. When Earth faces the Sun, it is ______________.

4. When Earth does not face the Sun, it is ______________.

Draw Conclusions

5. Look at the picture and tell if Earth is or is not facing the Sun.

I know		I conclude
	→	

Name ______________________________

Use with pages 324–327.

What is in the night sky?

Before You Read Lesson 3

Read each sentence. Do you think it is true? Do you think it is not true? Circle the word or words after each sentence that tell what you think.

1. Stars do not move across the night sky.	True	Not True
2. Earth moves around the Sun.	True	Not True
3. The Moon gives off light.	True	Not True

After You Read Lesson 3

Read each sentence again. Circle the word or words after each sentence that tell what you think now. Did you change any answers? Put an **X** by each answer that you changed.

1. Stars do not move across the night sky.	True	Not True
2. Earth moves around the Sun.	True	Not True
3. The Moon gives off light.	True	Not True

© Pearson Education, Inc.

Home Activity: Together talk about your child's answers. Have your child explain why his or her answers may have changed after reading the lesson.

Name ______________________________

Use with pages 324–327.

Complete the Sentence

Write the word that completes each sentence.

planet	Moon	light	telescope

1. Earth is called a ______________.

2. You can use a ______________ to see things in the night sky.

3. The ______________ is in the sky but is not like Earth.

4. The ______________ from the Sun can help us see things in the sky.

Important Details

5. Write two important details about what is in the sky.

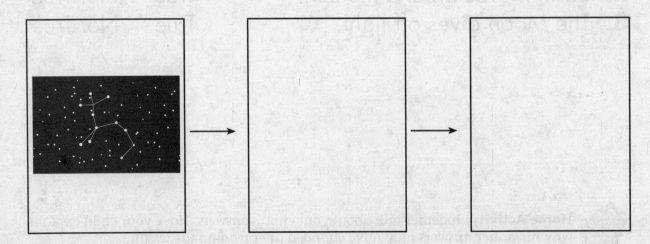

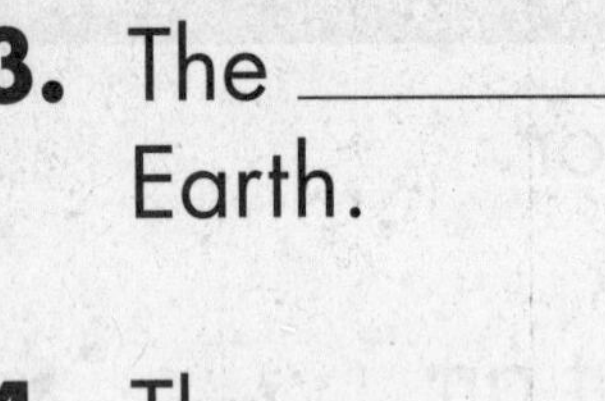

→ [ ] → [ ]

Name ______________________________ **Math** in Science

Use with Chapter 11.

Reading a Calendar

Every night Sophia looks at the night sky.
This is her calendar for July.
Sophia writes M when she sees the Moon.
She writes S when she sees the stars.

July						
Sunday	**Monday**	**Tuesday**	**Wednesday**	**Thursday**	**Friday**	**Saturday**
				1 M S	2 M S	3 M S
4 M S	5	6	7 S	8 S	9	10
11	12 M S	13 M S	14 M S	15	16 S	17 S
18 S	19	20	21 M	22 M	23	24
25	26	27	28	29 M S	30 M S	31 M S

Use the calendar to answer the questions.

1. Sophia saw the Moon on July 4. How many nights passed before she saw the Moon again? ______________________

2. Sophia saw the stars on July 18. How many nights passed before she saw the stars again? ______________________

© Pearson Education, Inc.

Directions: Remember that M stands for Moon and S stands for stars. To answer each question, find the date and then count the nights until you see the next M or S. **Home Activity:** Your child learned how to read a calendar. Look at a calendar for the current month. Ask your child questions about the calendar, such as *How many days does this month have? How many Thursdays are there? What day does the 26th fall on?*

Notes

Family Science Activity

Exploring Day and Night

Materials
- Ball
- Flashlight
- Sticky note

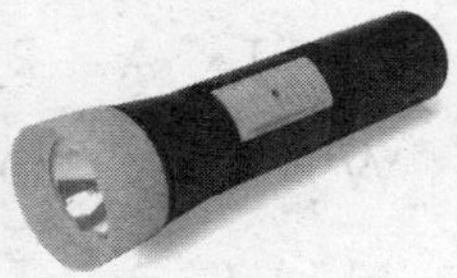

Steps
1. Tell your child that the ball is a model of Earth. Have your child place the sticky note on one side of the ball.
2. Hold the ball at the top and at the bottom. Show your child how to model Earth's rotation by spinning the ball.
3. Give the ball to your child to spin. Shine a flashlight at the ball.
4. Ask your child to identify when the light strikes the sticky note. As the ball rotates, the sticky note will move in and out of the light.
5. Talk with your child about how this activity models Earth's rotation, causing day and night.

© Pearson Education, Inc.

Dear Family,

In the science chapter Day and Night Sky, our class is learning about objects in the day and night sky. The children have studied about the Sun and the Moon. We have also learned about Earth's rotation and how it causes day and night. Further, the children explored stars, planets, and the Moon in the night sky.

In addition to learning about the day and night sky, the children have also learned many new vocabulary words. Help your child to make these words a part of his or her own vocabulary by using them when you talk together about objects in the sky.

Sun
Moon
rotation
star
planet
telescope

The following pages include activities that you and your child can do together. By participating in your child's education, you will help to bring the learning home.

What's in the Sky?

Draw a line from the object to the words that tell about it.

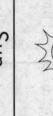

Sun

Moon

planet

hard to see in the day sky

hot ball of gas

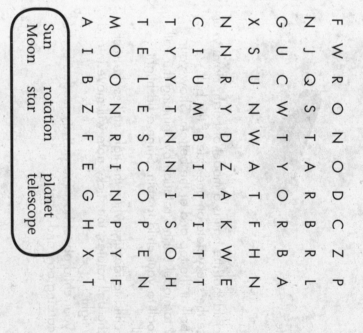

moves around the Sun

© Pearson Education, Inc.

Sky Search

Circle the words in the puzzle.

F	W	R	O	N	O	D	C	Z	P
N	J	Q	S	T	A	R	B	R	L
G	U	C	W	T	Y	O	R	B	A
X	S	U	N	W	A	T	F	H	N
N	N	R	Y	D	Z	A	K	W	E
C	I	U	M	B	I	T	I	T	T
T	Y	Y	T	N	N	I	S	O	H
T	E	L	E	S	C	O	P	E	N
M	O	O	N	R	I	N	P	Y	F
A	I	B	Z	F	E	G	H	X	T

Sun	rotation	planet
Moon	star	telescope

Fun Fact

Galileo was a famous scientist. Galileo used a telescope to study the sky. People used to think that the Moon was smooth. Galileo saw that the Moon was bumpy.

Name ________________________________

Use with Chapter 12.

Draw a picture or write a sentence to go with each word.

technology	pulley
simple machine	incline plane
wedge	screw
wheel and axle	lever

© Pearson Education, Inc.

Directions: Read the words and draw pictures to illustrate them or write sentences about them. Cut out the boxes to use as word cards.
Home Activity: Arrange the word cards in hierarchical order, with *technology* at the top, *simple machines* below that, and the six simple machines below that. Discuss with your child how each row is related to the row above.

Name ______________________________

How to Read Science

Use with Chapter 12.

Put Things in Order

Read the sentences.
Look at the pictures.

Science Diagram

Allie planted a vegetable garden. First, she planted three tomato plants. Next, she planted two zucchini plants. Then she planted four bean plants. Last, she planted six pepper plants.

Pepper plants

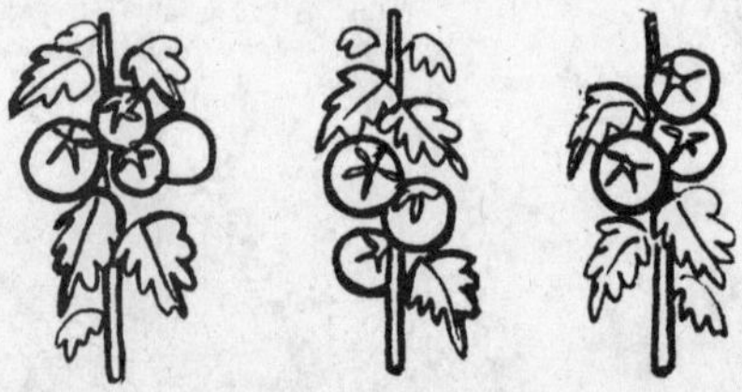

Tomato plants

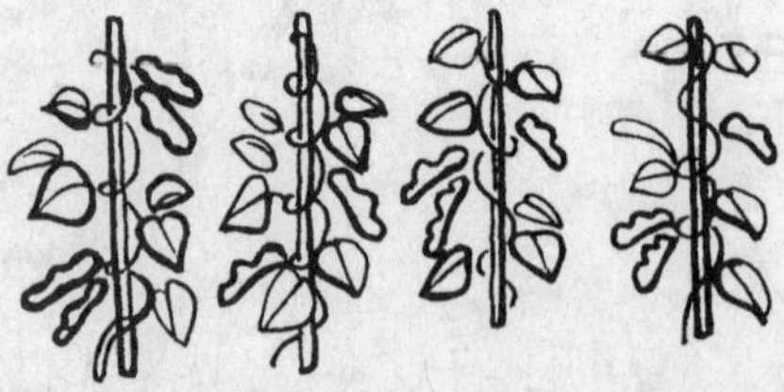

Bean plants

Zucchini plants

© Pearson Education, Inc.

Name ______________________________

Apply It!

Communicate Look at the pictures on page 124. Tell which vegetables were planted *first*, *next*, *then*, and *last*.

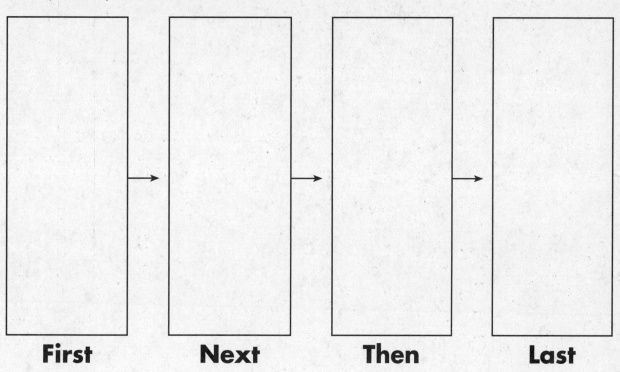

First → **Next** → **Then** → **Last**

© Pearson Education, Inc.

Directions: Read the sentences. Think about what happens first, next, then, and last. Decide how you would put the pictures in order.
Home Activity: Your child learned about the concept of sequence, or putting things in the order in which they happen. Point to each picture on the page and ask your child to tell how he or she decided whether that picture showed what happens first, next, then, or last.

Notes

Name ______________________

Use with pages 343–345.

How do farmers use technology to grow food?

Before You Read Lesson 1

Read each sentence. Do you think it is true? Do you think it is not true? Circle the word or words after each sentence that tell what you think.

1. Some foods come from farm animals and crops. True Not True

2. Technology makes work harder to do. True Not True

3. A plow is an example of technology. True Not True

After You Read Lesson 1

Read each sentence again. Circle the word or words after each sentence that tell what you think now. Did you change any answers? Put an **X** by each answer that you changed.

1. Some foods come from farm animals and crops. True Not True

2. Technology makes work harder to do. True Not True

3. A plow is an example of technology. True Not True

© Pearson Education, Inc.

Home Activity: Together talk about your child's answers. Have your child explain why his or her answers may have changed after reading the lesson.

Name ________________________

Use with pages 343–345.

Complete the Sentence

Write the word that completes each sentence.

plant	food	changes	technology

1. We use some crops for ____________.

2. Farmers use ____________ to help them do their work.

3. A machine helps farmers ____________ corn.

4. Technology ____________ over time.

Picture Clues

5. Use picture clues and color the picture of the plant we use as food.

Plant 1	Plant 2	Plant 3
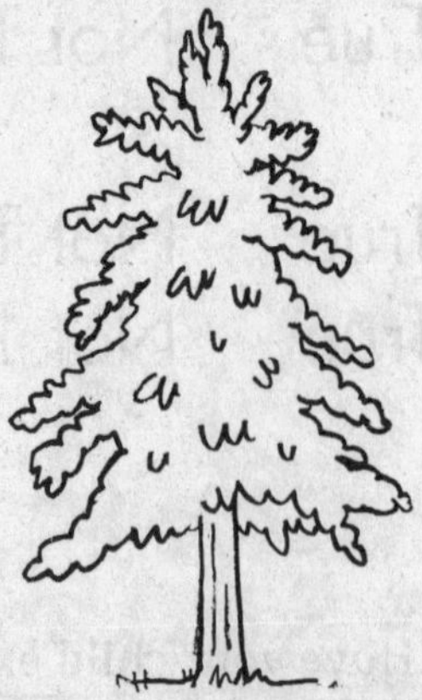		

Name ______________________________

Use with pages 346–347.

How does food get from the farm to the store?

Before You Read Lesson 2

Read each sentence. Do you think it is true? Do you think it is not true? Circle the word or words after each sentence that tell what you think.

1. Farmers grow corn plants from seeds. True Not True
2. Farmers pick corn by hand. True Not True
3. Trucks take corn from the farm to stores. True Not True

After You Read Lesson 2

Read each sentence again. Circle the word or words after each sentence that tell what you think now. Did you change any answers? Put an **X** by each answer that you changed.

1. Farmers grow corn plants from seeds. True Not True
2. Farmers pick corn by hand. True Not True
3. Trucks take corn from the farm to stores. True Not True

Home Activity: Together talk about your child's answers. Have your child explain why his or her answers may have changed after reading the lesson.

© Pearson Education, Inc.

Name ______________________

Use with pages 346–347.

Complete the Sentence

Write the word that completes each sentence.

store	pick	farmer	truck

1. A ____________ is a person who grows corn and other crops.

2. A machine is used to ____________ the corn.

3. The corn is put into a ____________.

4. Then the corn goes to a ____________, and people buy it.

Important Details

5. Write two important details you learned about how people are able to buy corn.

Name ______________________________

Use with pages 348–351.

What tools can you use to make dinner?

Before You Read Lesson 3

Read each sentence. Do you think it is true? Do you think it is not true? Circle the word or words after each sentence that tell what you think.

1.	Different tools do different jobs.	True	Not True
2.	You can use scissors to cut things.	True	Not True
3.	A knife is used to stir things.	True	Not True

After You Read Lesson 3

Read each sentence again. Circle the word or words after each sentence that tell what you think now. Did you change any answers? Put an **X** by each answer that you changed.

1.	Different tools do different jobs.	True	Not True
2.	You can use scissors to cut things.	True	Not True
3.	A knife is used to stir things.	True	Not True

© Pearson Education, Inc.

Home Activity: Together talk about your child's answers. Have your child explain why his or her answers may have changed after reading the lesson.

Name ______________________

Use with pages 348–351.

Complete the Sentence

Write the word that completes each sentence.

make	spoon	serve	work

1. With tools, it is easier to do __________.

2. A __________ is a kind of tool.

3. You can use many tools to __________ a meal for your family.

4. You use different tools to help you __________ a meal.

Alike and Different

5. Write how the tools below are alike and different.

is a tool   is sharp   is not sharp   used to eat with

Spoon	Fork
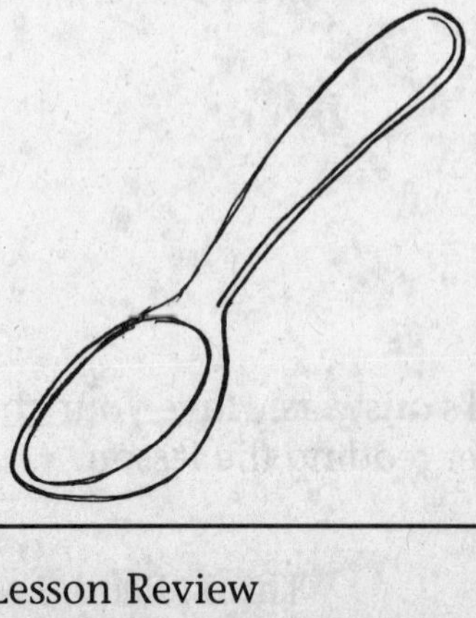	

Name ______________________________

Use with pages 352–355.

How do builders get wood for a house?

Before You Read Lesson 4

Read each sentence. Do you think it is true? Do you think it is not true? Circle the word or words after each sentence that tell what you think.

1. Today loggers use axes to cut down trees. True Not True
2. Trucks take logs to a sawmill. True Not True
3. Logs are cut into boards at a sawmill. True Not True

After You Read Lesson 4

Read each sentence again. Circle the word or words after each sentence that tell what you think now. Did you change any answers? Put an **X** by each answer that you changed.

1. Today loggers use axes to cut down trees. True Not True
2. Trucks take logs to a sawmill. True Not True
3. Logs are cut into boards at a sawmill. True Not True

© Pearson Education, Inc.

Home Activity: Together talk about your child's answers. Have your child explain why his or her answers may have changed after reading the lesson.

Name ______________________

Lesson 4 Review

Use with pages 352–355.

Complete the Sentence

Write the word that completes each sentence.

sawmill	technology	ax	logs

1. Today, loggers use new __________ to cut down trees.

2. A long time ago, a logger would use an __________ to cut down a tree.

3. After trees are cut down, they are called __________.

4. The trees are then moved to a __________.

Put Things in Order

5. Put the pictures in order to show how trees end up being part of a house. Write "first," "second," "third," and "last" under the pictures.

__________ __________ __________ __________

Name ______________________________

Use with pages 356–359.

What are simple machines?

Before You Read Lesson 5

Read each sentence. Do you think it is true? Do you think it is not true? Circle the word or words after each sentence that tell what you think.

1. A simple machine has few or no moving parts. True Not True
2. A screw helps lift something. True Not True
3. A pulley is used to move things up and down. True Not True

After You Read Lesson 5

Read each sentence again. Circle the word or words after each sentence that tell what you think now. Did you change any answers? Put an **X** by each answer that you changed.

1. A simple machine has few or no moving parts. True Not True
2. A screw helps lift something. True Not True
3. A pulley is used to move things up and down. True Not True

© Pearson Education, Inc.

Home Activity: Together talk about your child's answers. Have your child explain why his or her answers may have changed after reading the lesson.

Name ______________________________

Use with pages 356–359.

Complete the Sentence

Write the word or phrase that completes each sentence.

simple machine	lever	inclined plane	screw

1. A ______________ is any tool with few parts.

2. A ______________ can hold things together.

3. Use a ______________ to lift something.

4. An ______________ is a ramp used to move things up and down.

Draw Conclusions

5. Look at the pictures and write why the people used an inclined plane.

I know		I conclude
	→	

Name ______________________________

Use with pages 360–361.

What can you use to communicate?

Before You Read Lesson 6

Read each sentence. Do you think it is true? Do you think it is not true? Circle the word or words after each sentence that tell what you think.

1.	We use technology to communicate with others.	True	Not True
2.	Technology never changes.	True	Not True
3.	We can send pictures by email.	True	Not True

After You Read Lesson 6

Read each sentence again. Circle the word or words after each sentence that tell what you think now. Did you change any answers? Put an **X** by each answer that you changed.

1.	We use technology to communicate with others.	True	Not True
2.	Technology never changes.	True	Not True
3.	We can send pictures by email.	True	Not True

© Pearson Education, Inc.

Home Activity: Together talk about your child's answers. Have your child explain why his or her answers may have changed after reading the lesson.

Name ______________________

Use with pages 360–361.

Complete the Sentence

Write the word that completes each sentence.

computer	technology	camera	radio

1. Different kinds of ____________ can be used to communicate.

2. A ____________ takes pictures to show things to other people.

3. A ____________ lets you hear different things.

4. With a ____________, you can write emails to friends.

Alike and Different

5. Write how the telephone and the computer are alike and different.

Telephone	**Computer**

Name ______________________________

Classifying Tools

You use different tools to do different jobs. But some tools can do more than one job. Look at the tools in the chart. Find out what job or jobs each tool can do.

Tools You Can Use		
To Cut	**To Lift**	**To Stir**
scissors	tongs	spatula
knife	spatula	large spoon
grater	large spoon	
	ladle	

Use the chart to answer these questions.

1. Does this chart show more tools for cutting or more tools for lifting?

____

2. Which tools can be used to do two different jobs? ______________________________

© Pearson Education, Inc.

Directions: The chart classifies, or groups, tools according to the jobs they can do. To find out which tools can do which jobs, read each column heading and look at the tools listed in that column. Use the information to answer the questions.
Home Activity: Your child learned how a chart can be used to classify things. Together make your own chart with three headings, such as *With Our Hands, With a Fork,* and *With a Spoon,* and classify foods according to which way or ways you can eat them.

Notes

Family Science Activity

Playground Machines

Materials
- Teeter-totter (at the playground)
- Slide (at the playground)

Steps
1. At the playground, ask your child if he or she can see any simple machines. Some simple machines are: levers, wedges, incline planes, and pulleys.
2. The teeter totter is a type of a lever. Set the teeter totter so that your child can lift you. As you use the teeter totter, talk about how the lever makes it easier for your child to lift you.
3. The slide is a type of incline plane. Have your child point out the high and low ends of the inclined plane.
4. Have your child name any other simple machine that may be found at the playground. For example, a Merry-Go-Round is a type of wheel and axle.

© Pearson Education, Inc.

Dear Family,

Your child is learning how technology is used in the world. In the science chapter Science in Our World, our class has learned how technology is used by farmers, in the kitchen, and by loggers. The children have also learned about simple machines. In addition, we learned how technology is used to help us communicate.

In addition to learning how technology is used in the world, the children have also learned many new vocabulary words. Help your child to make these words a part of his or her own vocabulary by using them when you talk together about how technology is used in the world.

technology
simple machine
wedge
wheel and axle
screw
lever
pulley
inclined plane

These following pages include activities that you and your child can do together. By participating in your child's education, you will help to bring the learning home.

Dinner Tools

Look at each tool.
Write how you can use each tool.

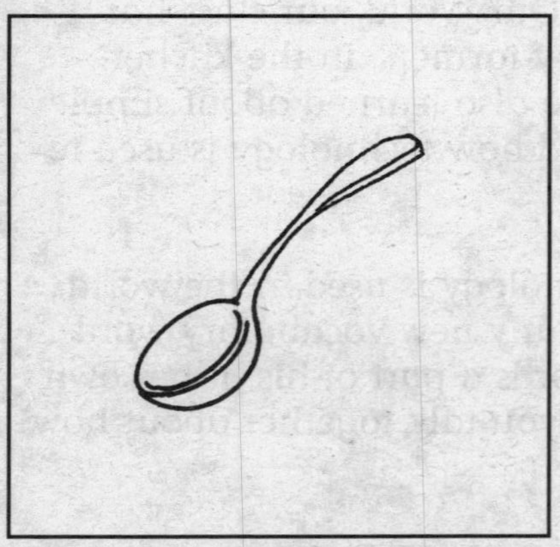

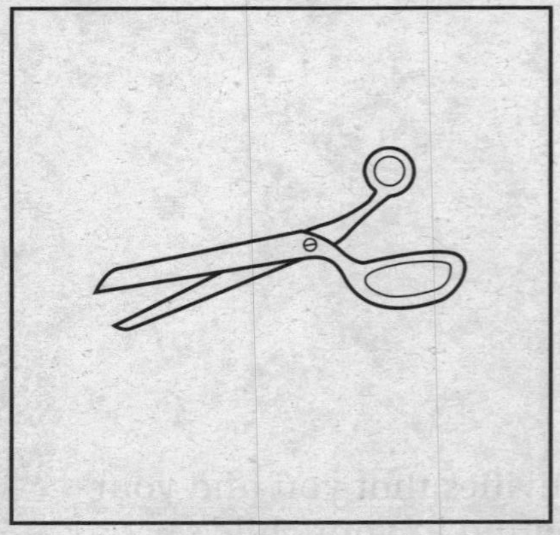

© Pearson Education, Inc.

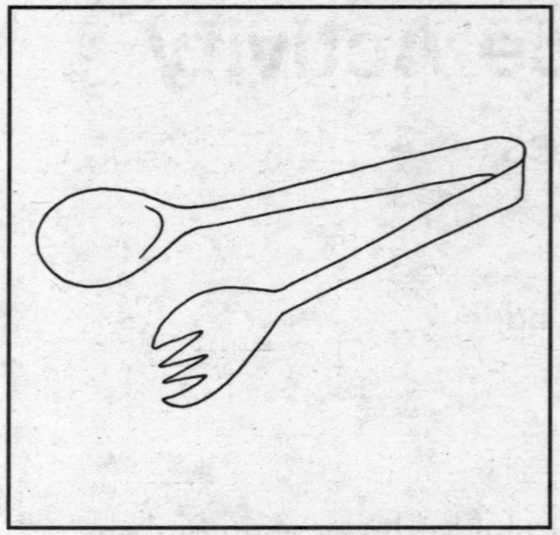

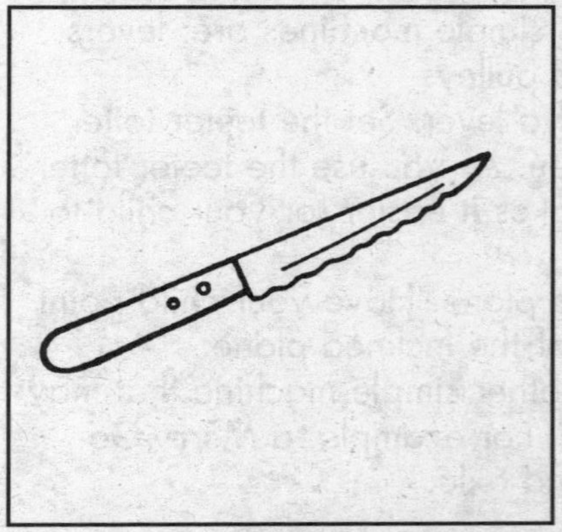

Name ______________________________

Use with Chapter 1, pp. 12–13

What do animals need?

Animals need food, water, and air. Animals need space to live. This is called shelter. The pictures below show animals meeting their needs.

The chipmunk is an animal. The chipmunk eats a flower for food.

The birds are young animals. The birds use a nest for shelter.

Answer these questions about the pictures above.

1. Is the chipmunk a plant or an animal? The chipmunk is an ________________ .
2. What does the chipmunk eat? The chipmunk eats a ________________ .
3. Why does the chipmunk eat a flower? The chipmunk needs ________________ .
4. The birds live in a ________________ .
5. The birds need a safe place to live. They use a nest for ________________ .

© Pearson Education, Inc.

Name ______________________

Use with Chapter 2, pp. 32–39

What are habitats?

Animals and plants live in habitats. A habitat has all of the things plants and animals need to live. There are many different kinds of habitats.

Habitats

Forest

Ocean

Wetland

Desert

Answer these questions.

1. What two habitats are made mostly of water? ______________

2. Which habitat is hot and dry? ________

3. What kinds of animals live in the ocean?

____

4. What things do plants and animals get from their habitats? ______________

© Pearson Education, Inc.

Name ________________________________

Use with Chapter 3, p. 58

How do animals get food?

Animals use parts of their body to get food. Some animals use sharp teeth. Other animals use claws. Birds use beaks to get food.

Two Kinds of Bird Beaks

Cardinal

Owl

Answer these questions.

1. How is the owl's beak different from the cardinal's beak?

____

2. How does a cardinal get food?

____

3. What kind of food does an owl eat?

____

4. What does the cardinal eat?

____

© Pearson Education, Inc.

Name ______________________

Use with Chapter 4, pp. 92–93

How does a butterfly grow?

A butterfly begins as an egg. A larva hatches from the egg. The larva becomes a pupa. The grown butterfly flies out of a pupa. The butterfly has wings to fly. It may lay eggs. The life cycle goes on.

Butterfly Life Cycle

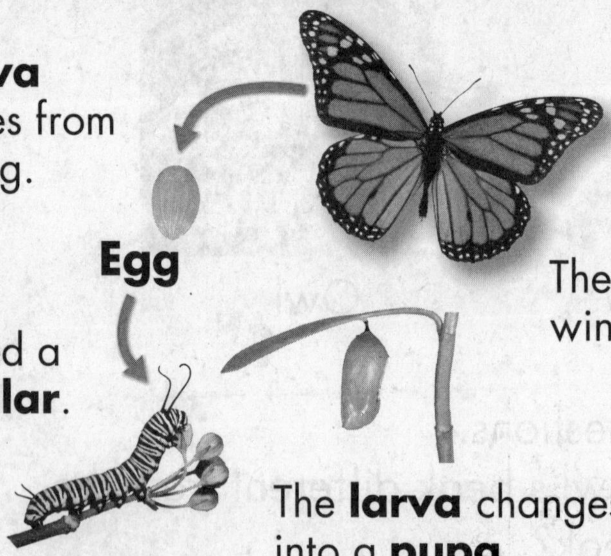
A **larva** hatches from the egg.
Egg
The **butterfly** has wings to fly.
It is called a **caterpillar**.
The **larva** changes into a **pupa**.

Answer these questions.

1. How many steps are there in a butterfly life cycle? ____

2. How does a butterfly begin its life? __________

3. What happens after the caterpillar hatches from the egg? __________________

4. How are the caterpillar and the butterfly different? ______________________________

____

____

© Pearson Education, Inc.

Name ______________________________

Use with Chapter 5, p. 125

What do animals eat?

Animals need food. Some animals eat plants. Some animals eat other animals. All living things are connected through food chains. This picture shows a food chain.

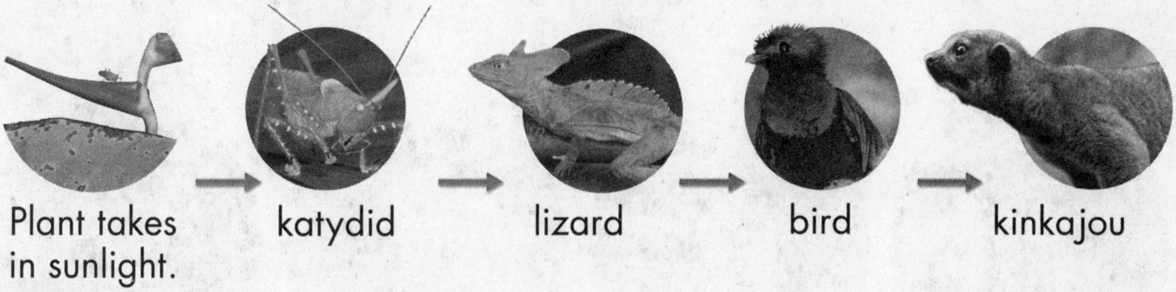

Answer these questions about the pictures.

1. Does the katydid eat plants or animals? The katydid eats ________.
2. What does the lizard eat? The lizard eats a ___________.
3. Why does the kinkajou eat the bird? The kinkajou needs ___________.
4. How does the plant make food? The plant takes in ___________ to make food.

© Pearson Education, Inc.

Name ______________________________

Using Science Pictures

Use with Chapter 6, pp. 152–153

What are some kinds of land and water?

Different kinds of land and water are found on Earth.

A **hill** is where the land gets higher.

A **plain** is flat land.

A **lake** has land all around it.

A **river** is water that flows through the land.

A **cliff** is very steep land.

Answer these questions.

1. What kind of land is flat? A ________ is flat land.
2. Where does the land get higher? A ________ is where the land gets higher.
3. What kind of water has land all around it? A ____________ has land all around it.
4. What kind of water flows through land? A ____________ flows through land.
5. What kind of land is steep? A ____________ is steep land.

© Pearson Education, Inc.

Name ______________________________

Use with Chapter 7, pp. 184–185

How is weather measured?

Tools are used to measure weather.

A **thermometer** measures temperature.

A **wind vane** shows the direction of the wind.

A **rain gauge** measures how much rain falls.

Write the missing word in each sentence below.

1. A ____________ shows the direction of the wind.

2. The ____________ shows a high temperature.

3. A ____________ measures how much rain falls.

© Pearson Education, Inc.

Name ______________________________ **Using Science Pictures**

Use with Chapter 8, pp. 222–223

How does matter change?

Matter can be changed in different ways. Look at the pictures and find things that have changed.

The straw was straight. Now the straw is bent.

The treat was frozen. Now it is melting because it is warm outside.

A whole apple has one shape but it can be cut into new shapes.

Answer the questions.

1. What changed when it was cut? The ____________ changed when it was cut.

2. How did the straw change? The straw is now ____________ .

3. What is melting? The ____________ is melting.

4. Why is the treat changing? It is changing because the temperature is ____________ .

5. What will happen to the ice if the cooler stays open? The ice will ____________ .

© Pearson Education, Inc.

Name ______________________________

Use with Chapter 9, pp. 252–253

How do things move?

Things move in different ways. Things can move up and down, right and left, or in a zigzag. Things can move straight or in a curve.

The marble rolls **straight** down the orange bar. Then it moves in a **zigzag**. It moves **down** the bars.

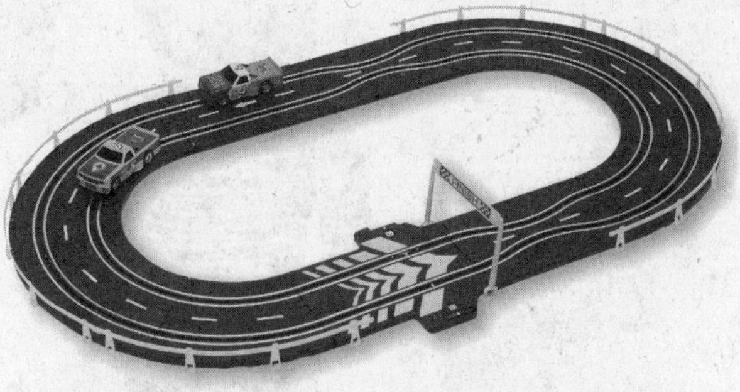

The cars go **around** a curve. Then, the cars go **straight**. Next, the cars turn around another **curve**.

Answer these questions.

1. Circle the ways the marble moves.

Zigzag   Straight   Down   Up

2. How do the cars move around the race track? First, the cars go around a ____________ . Then, the cars go ____________ . Next, the cars turn around another ________ .

© Pearson Education, Inc.

Name ______________________________

Use with Chapter 10, pp. 286–287

How is a shadow made?

Light passes through some things. It will pass through a window, but not a toy. A shadow is made when something blocks the light.

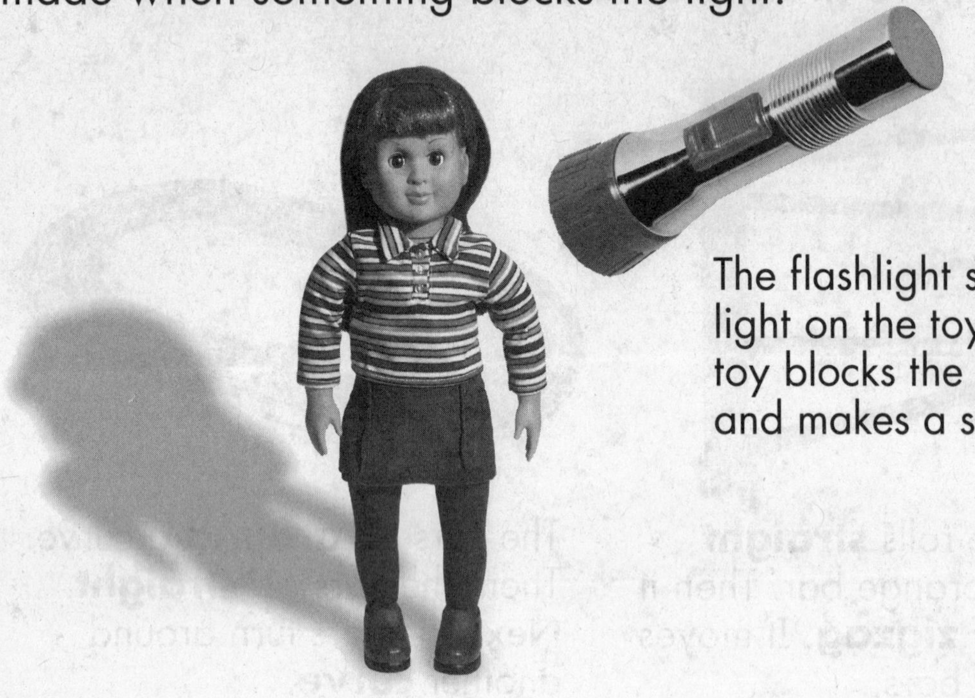

The flashlight shines light on the toy. The toy blocks the light and makes a shadow.

A shadow is large when the light is close. A shadow is small when the light is far away.

Complete the sentences.

1. The light comes from the __________ .

2. The ___________ blocks the light.

3. A ___________ is made when light is blocked.

4. The shadow is large when the light is ________ .

5. The shadow is small when the light is ________ .

© Pearson Education, Inc.

Name ______________________________

Use with Chapter 11, pp. 324–326

What is in the night sky?

Stars	Planets	Moon
		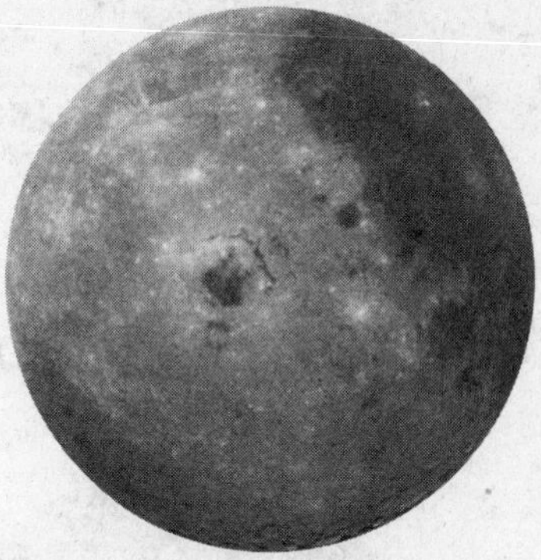
A star is a ball of hot gas. Stars give off light.	Planets move around the Sun. Earth is a planet.	The Moon moves around Earth. The Moon has no air.

Complete these sentences about the night sky.

1. ____________ give off light in the night sky.

2. Earth is a ____________ .

3. The ____________ moves around Earth.

© Pearson Education, Inc.

Name ______________________________ **Using Science Pictures**

Use with Chapter 12, pp. 357–358

What are simple machines?

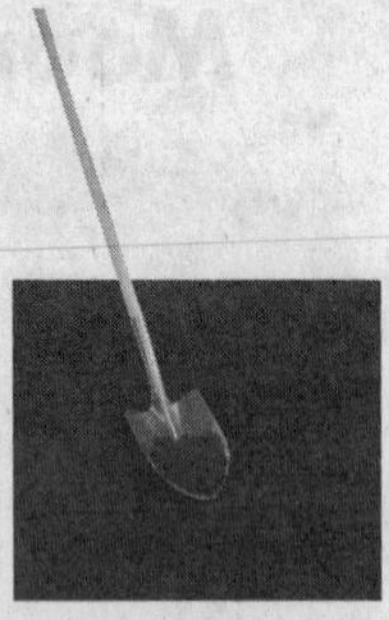

This **shovel** is a kind of wedge. A wedge pushes things apart.

This **wheelbarrow** has a wheel and axle. A wheel and axle is used to move things.

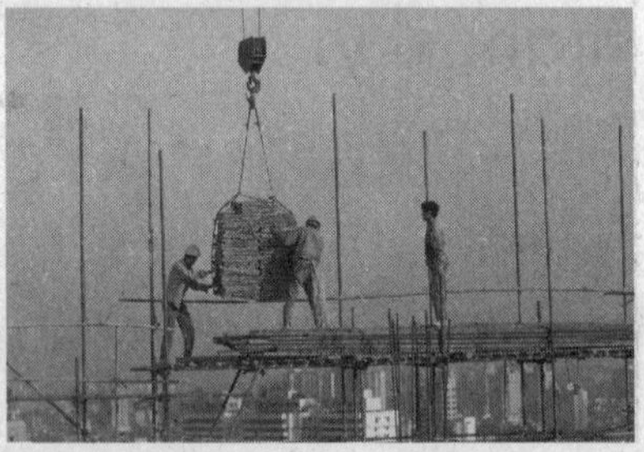

This **crane** uses a **pulley**. A pulley moves things up and down.

Answer these questions about the pictures.

1. What tool pushes things apart?
A ____________ pushes things apart.

2. Which tool has a wheel and axle?
A ____________ has a wheel and axle.

3. What direction does a pulley move things?
A pulley moves things ____________ and ____________ .

4. What kind of simple machine is a shovel? A shovel is a ______________ .

© Pearson Education, Inc.

Notes

Notes

Notes

Notes

Notes

Notes